LINOGLYPHIC ART

Introducing a New Art Form

by

Bobby Keyes, PhD

Linoglyphic Art copyright © 2013 Robert E. Keyes, Jr.

DEDICATION

This book of artwork is dedicated to the glory of God, Lorbor W., Mark B., Tiffany P., Khushroo G. Sam C., and to the memory of Rembrandt van Rijn.

TABLE OF CONTENTS

Introduction
The Finger Works
The Pencil Works
Postscript

Introduction

Linoglyphic Art was conceived as a response to a challenge to KEYES who had been struggling to recreate the insightful genius of Rembrandt. After displaying remarkable talent in the portraiture genre, KEYES was still dissatisfied. It seemed that he was merely restating the obvious. During a session of self-deprecation, a friend of the artist challenged KEYES "just try painting what you feel".

Abhorring the fanciful vision of a tortured spirit splashing paint on the canvas and swirling the brush madly in tormented spasms of so-called creativity, KEYES was in a quandary. How does one paint a feeling? Later that night in the throes of a fitful night's sleep, the ghost of Rembrandt appeared to KEYES as if standing in his studio in Amsterdam. The ghost of Rembrandt hurled a pot of blue paint against the wall. The paint obliterated the studio and the ghost faded away wearing an impish smirk of defiance that taunted KEYES to become original. The message was clear: stop trying to be Rembrandt and start being KEYES.

The next afternoon, KEYES sat in his garage furiously smoking a cigar while pondering the dream. With a pencil, KEYES sketched out the first linoglyph "Dream". After "Dream" was composed, a string of spontaneously obsessive sessions led to the compositions found in this groundbreaking book.

"After I composed 'Dream', I searched the Internet on different ideas about line art, minimalism, and other associated ideas to see if I was subconsciously duplicated something I had seen before", said KEYES in a recent interview. "I discovered similarities of my linoglyphs with the work of Pablo Picasso and Al Hirschfeld, but in no way was I copying these titans of the art world. I concluded that I had achieved originality as Rembrandt had challenged me. I dubbed my new art form *linoglyphs*."

Linoglyph is a hybrid word combining the words *line* and *hieroglyph.* Each linoglyph is accompanied by a word that merely suggests the cognitive connotation of the line drawing. Each linoglyph evokes a universal human experience. Although the words are English in this volume of linoglypghs, they could be translated to any other language without weakening the effects of the drawing.

Linoglypghs immediately penetrate the human psyche and resonate across cultures and space-time. "Linoglyphs are mesmerizing and unforgettable. They are spontaneous creations taking no more than a few minutes to compose," said KEYES. "Even I cannot duplicate one of my own linoglyphs. For instance, notice the difference in the linoglyphs for *hate* and *obese.* The present moment being experienced affects the cognitive state of mind and spawns unique results. This is the essence and power of linoglyphic art: the melding of spontaneous fleeting mental machinations with minimalist art techniques. Entirely different results occur under various psychological states".

Linoglyphs are not 'doodling', which implies vacuous idiocy. Linoglyphs are the spontaneous free flow of consciousness. The inner mind is linked directly to the point of the drawing instrument. The lines are drawn in response to a focused mental concentration on a thought, feeling, emotion, or idea. No preconception of the image occurs. The result is a unique image that cannot be recreated except by forgery or copying. A linoglyph is a visual artistic utterance of the sentient brain. A linoglyph is abrupt and unplanned. "Rarely do I erase the first effort of composing a linoglyph", said KEYES. "To erase the initial effort is to destroy the essence of spontaneity. I might not like how my linoglyphs looks, but that is the charm of this art from. I do not expect or even care what someone else thinks about my linoglyphs. They are mine, and I am a genius, and this is what my genius looks like."

Most of the linoglypghs in this book were drawn with No.2 pencil on 8½" by 11" plain white copier paper. A few were drawn by finger on a touchscreen tablet. One was drawn using a brush pen with India ink. No attempt has been made to alter the linoglyphs from their original state by trickery with photo editing. The images in this book are as close to their genuine spontaneous nature as possible. "As each individual has an individual style of hand-writing, so it is with linoglyphic art. My particular style is evident in my works. Another linoglyphic artist's style would be different than mine. However, I invented this art form, so all others will be compared to my superior original style", said KEYES.

This introduction volume of KEYES linoglyphs is presented mostly in reverse chronological order of their creation. No meaning should be implied as to the order or sequencing of the linoglyphs. Indeed, such ordering is impossible because of the erratic and spontaneous nature of this art form. Each linoglyph should be studied in detail to discover the nuance of each line, swirl, swell, or mark. Some semblance to human form is apparent in the linoglyphs but is coincidental to the spirit by which they were created.

KEYES linoglyphs are available for licensing for imprinting on objects such as T-shirts, coffee cups, and other promotional items. KEYES might also consider commissioning of personalized linoglyphs or hand-signed reproductions of the originals. Contact the author Bobby Keyes at KEYES@linoglyph.com for information about licensing reproductions of any particular KEYES linoglyph.

KEYES is a phantom-like artist reporting only to the author Bobby Keyes. KEYES occasionally reveals his talents through works of visual art, most recently in these astonishing linoglyphs. KEYES is a genius of profound insight, intelligence, and surprising inventiveness. "I will reveal my work only through Bobby Keyes, who has my express permission to publish all my efforts."

The Finger Works

The simplicity of linoglyphic art lends itself to production by many different means and in many different media. Although originally conceived using a graphite pencil, KEYES found that the essence and expression of linoglyphic art could be expressed using a touchscreen tablet device. The lines are less crisp and the linoglyphs less complex when rendered with a finger on a touchscreen. Nevertheless, the results are startling and oftentimes more profound than if a pencil had been used.

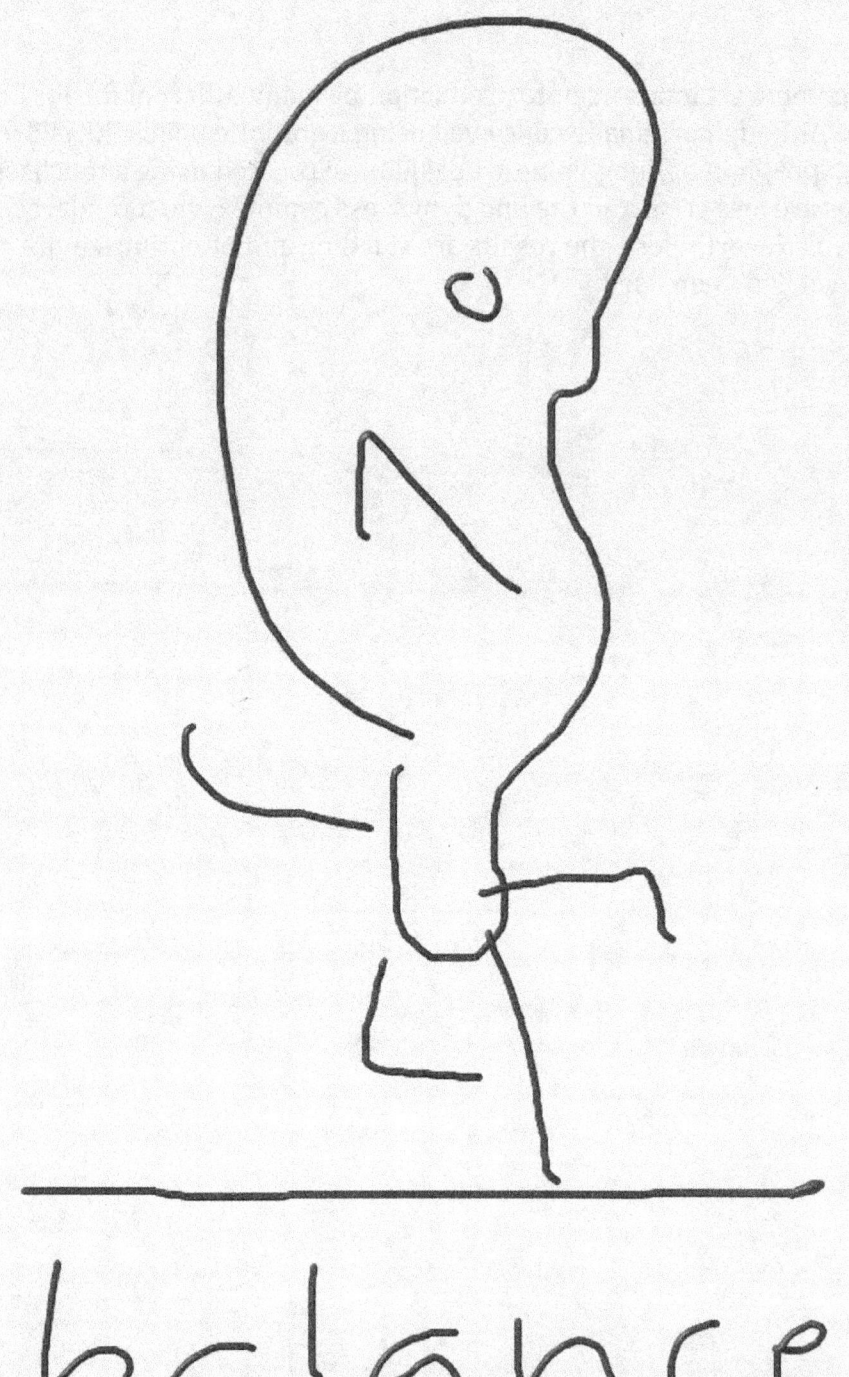

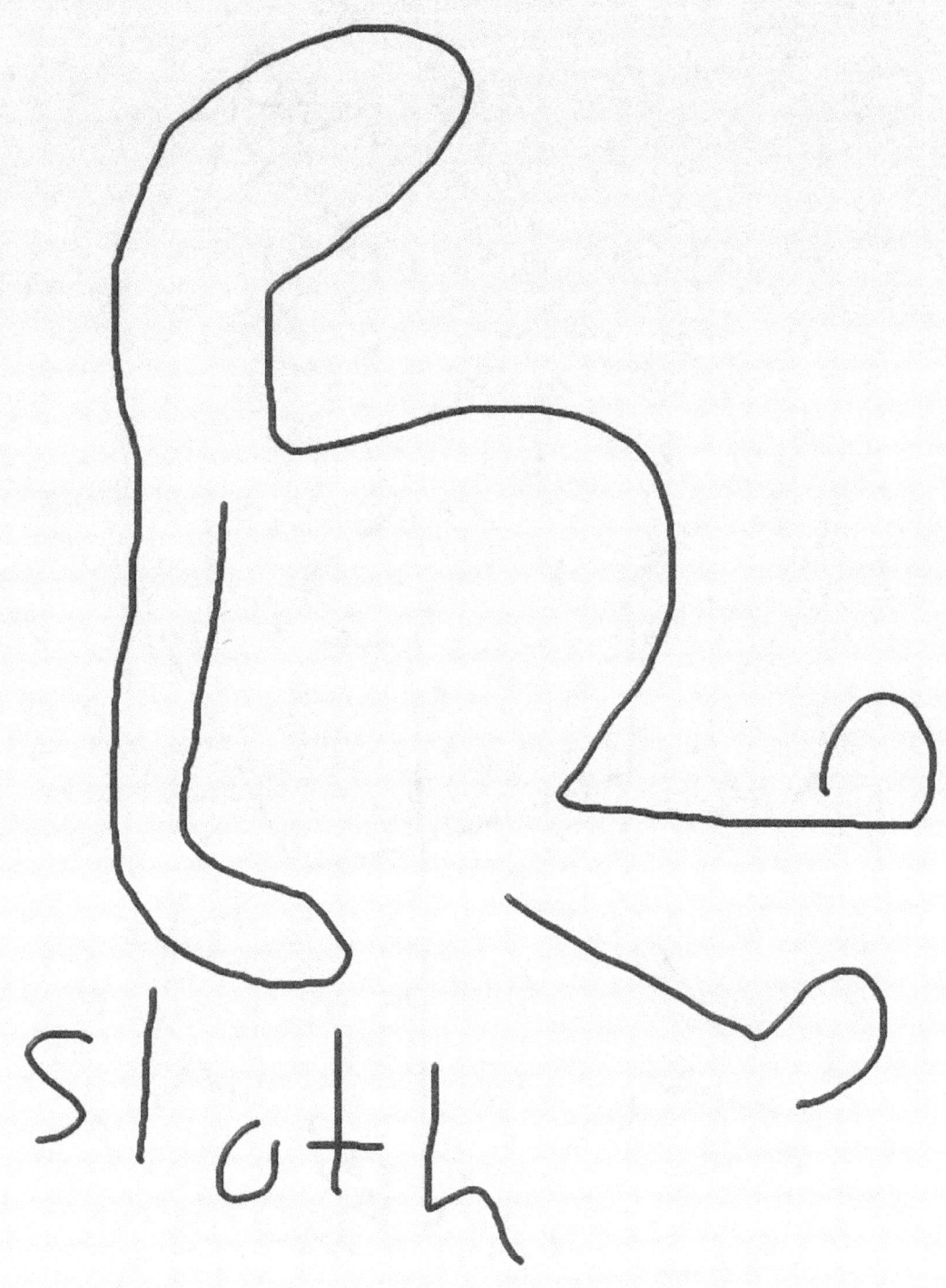

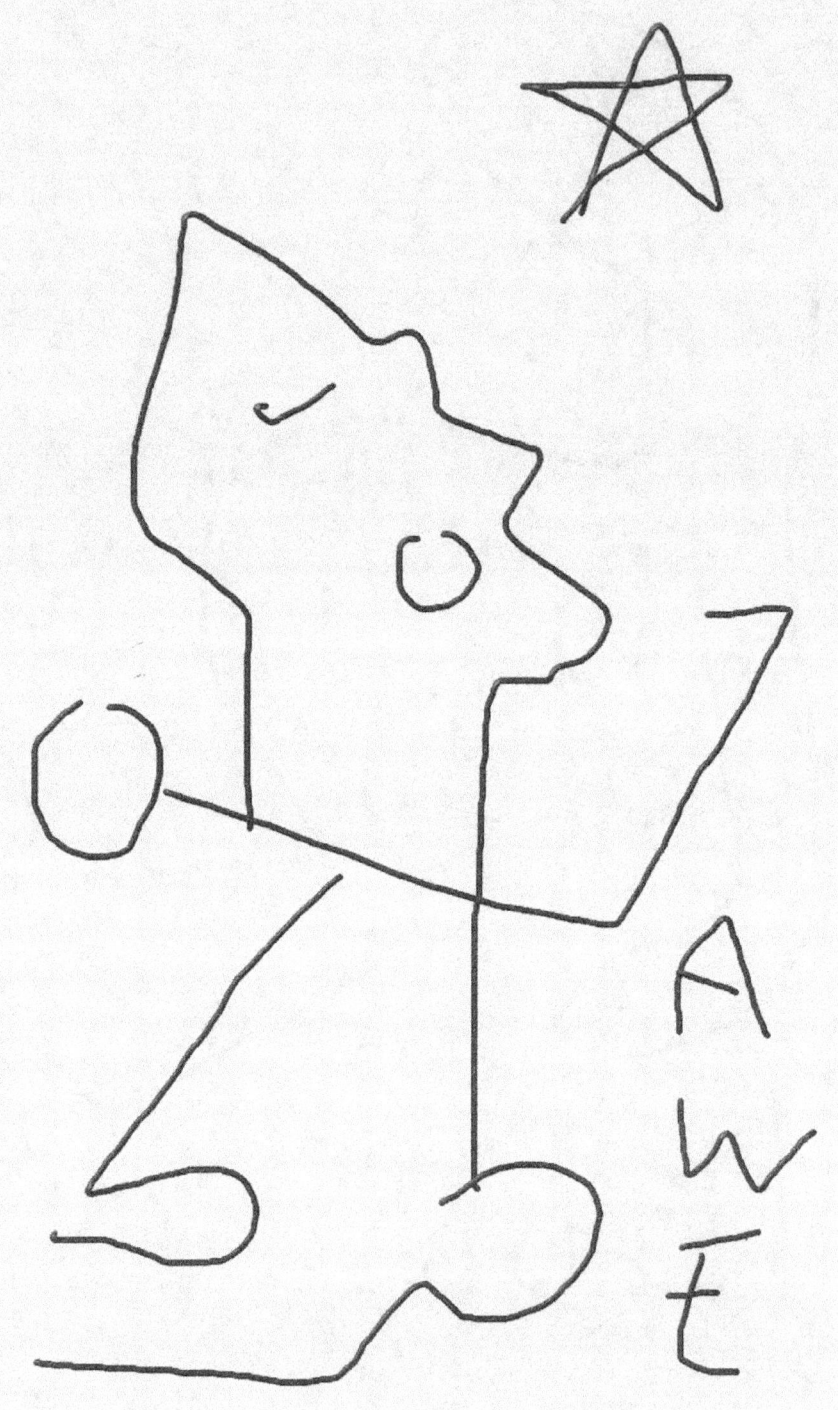

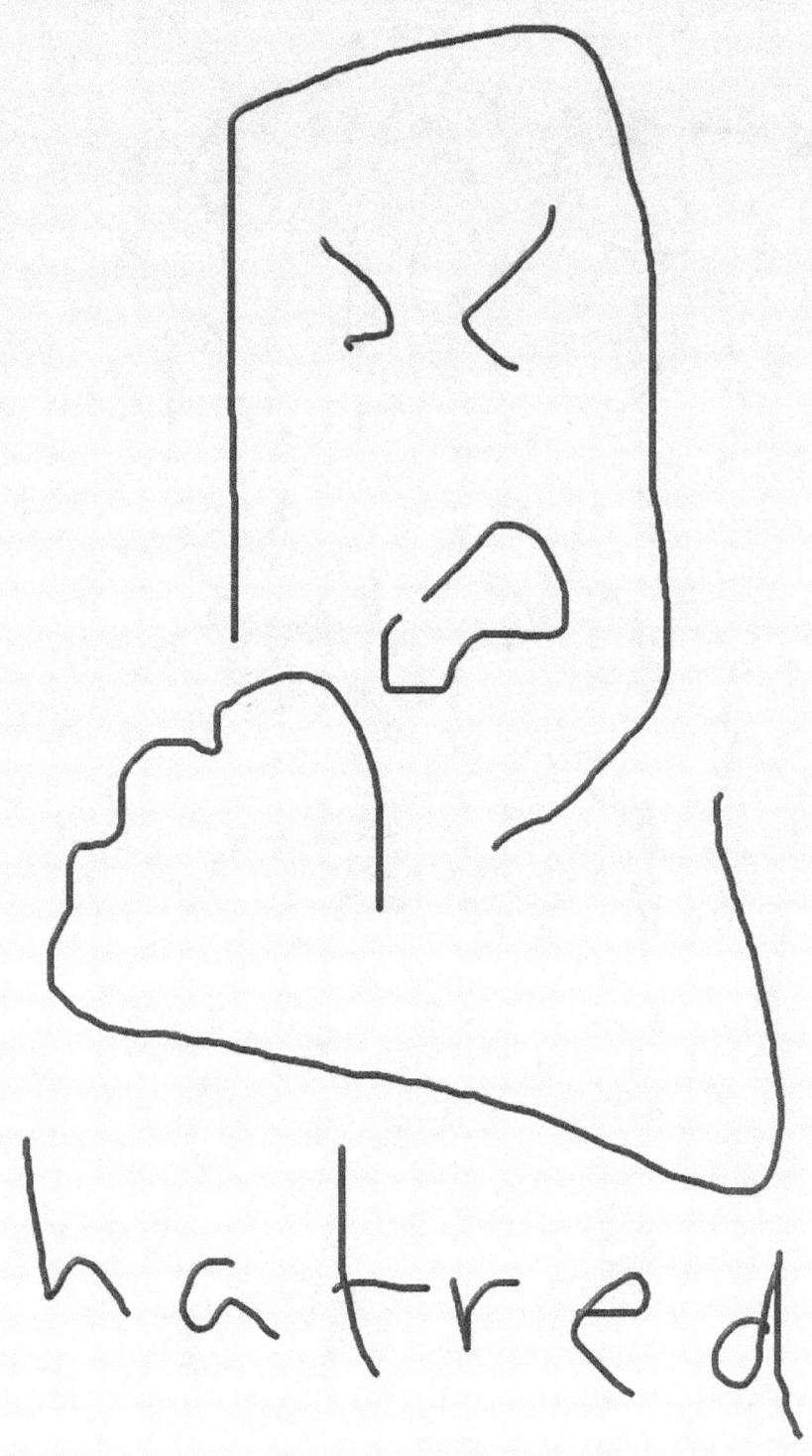

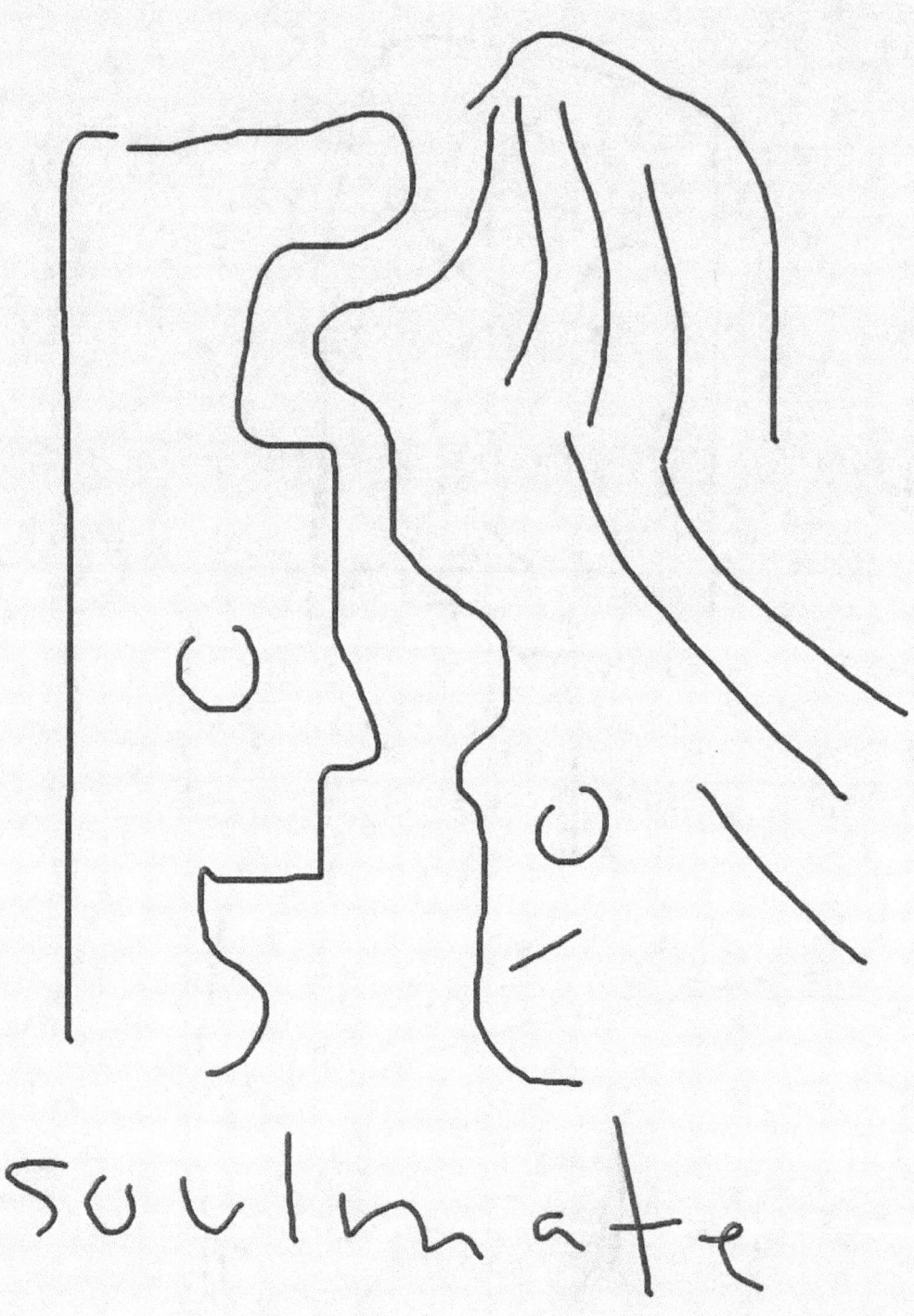

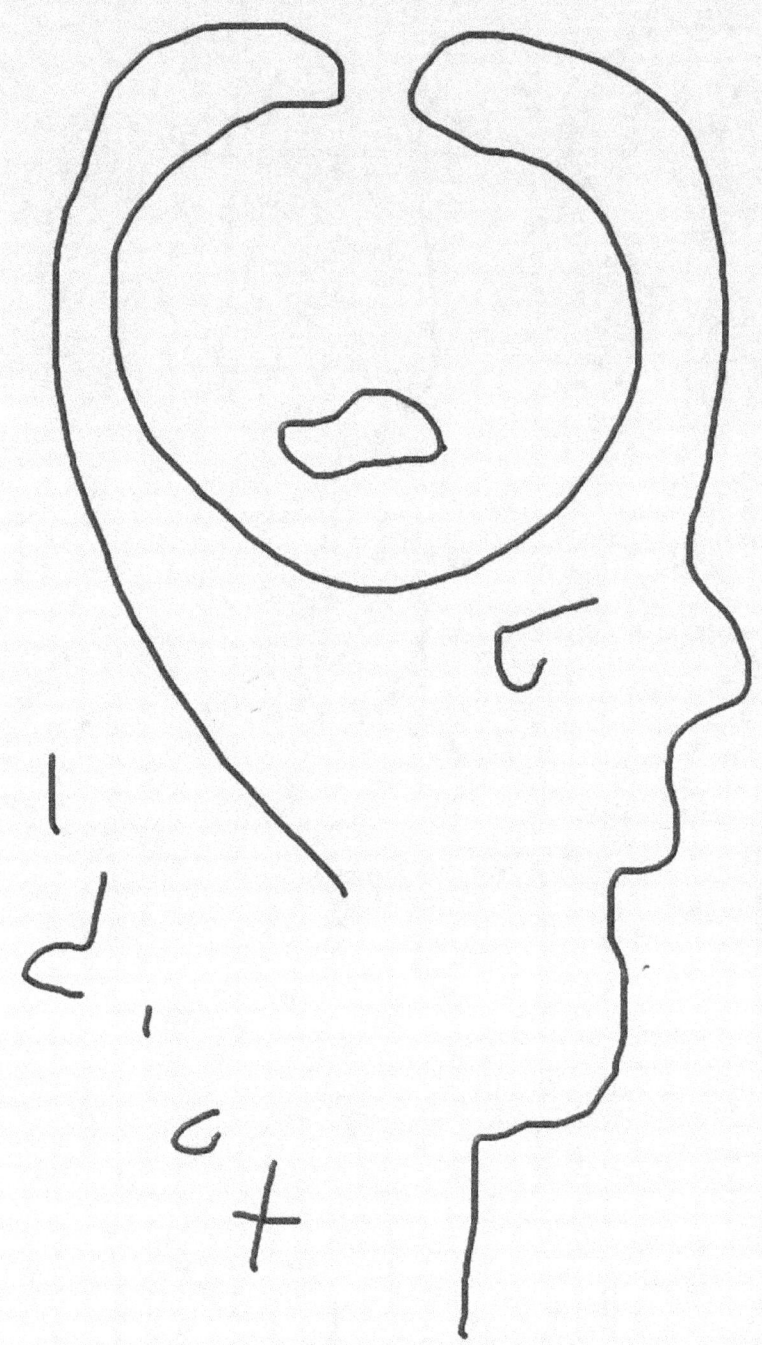

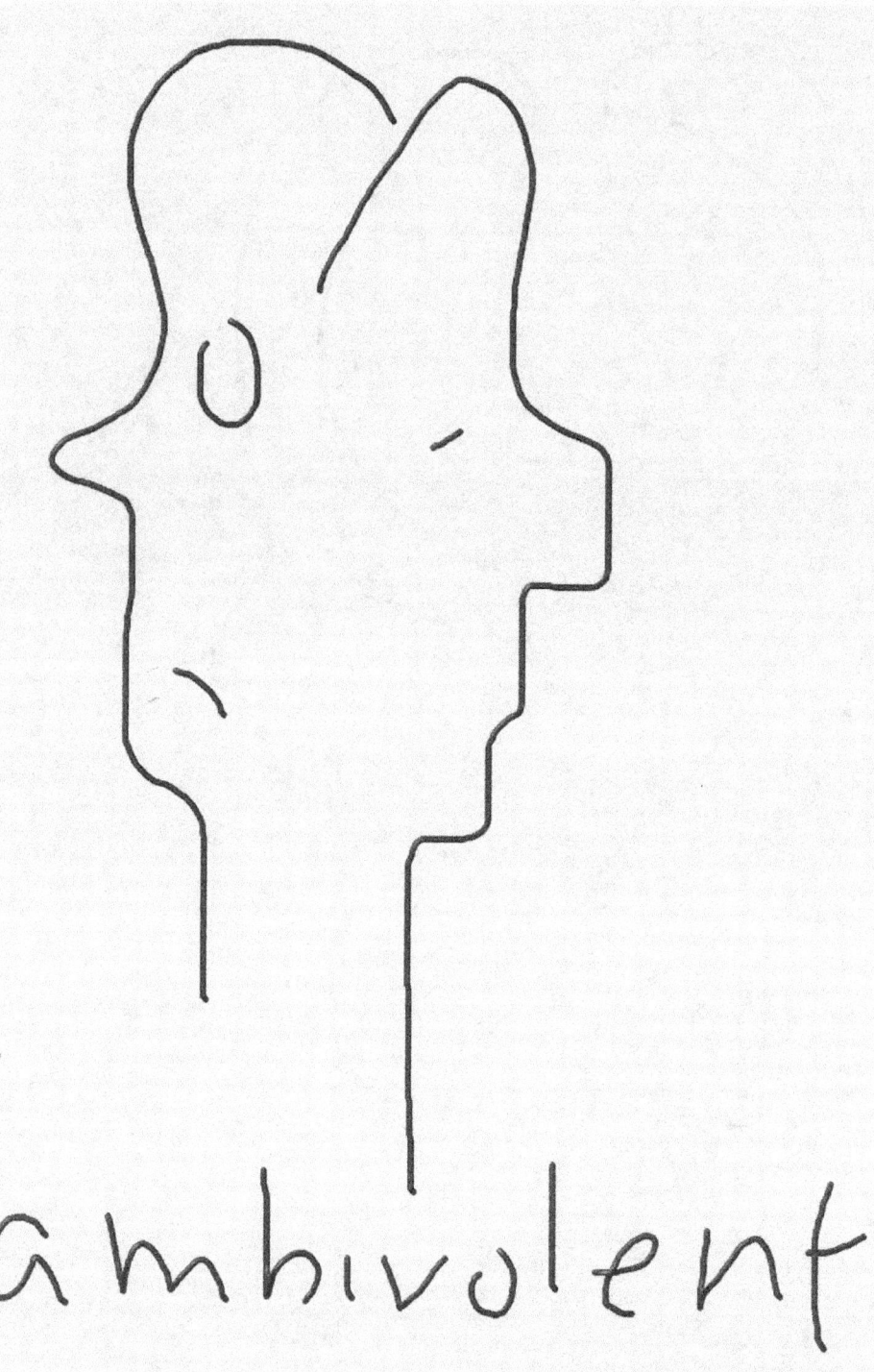

obese

10/15/13

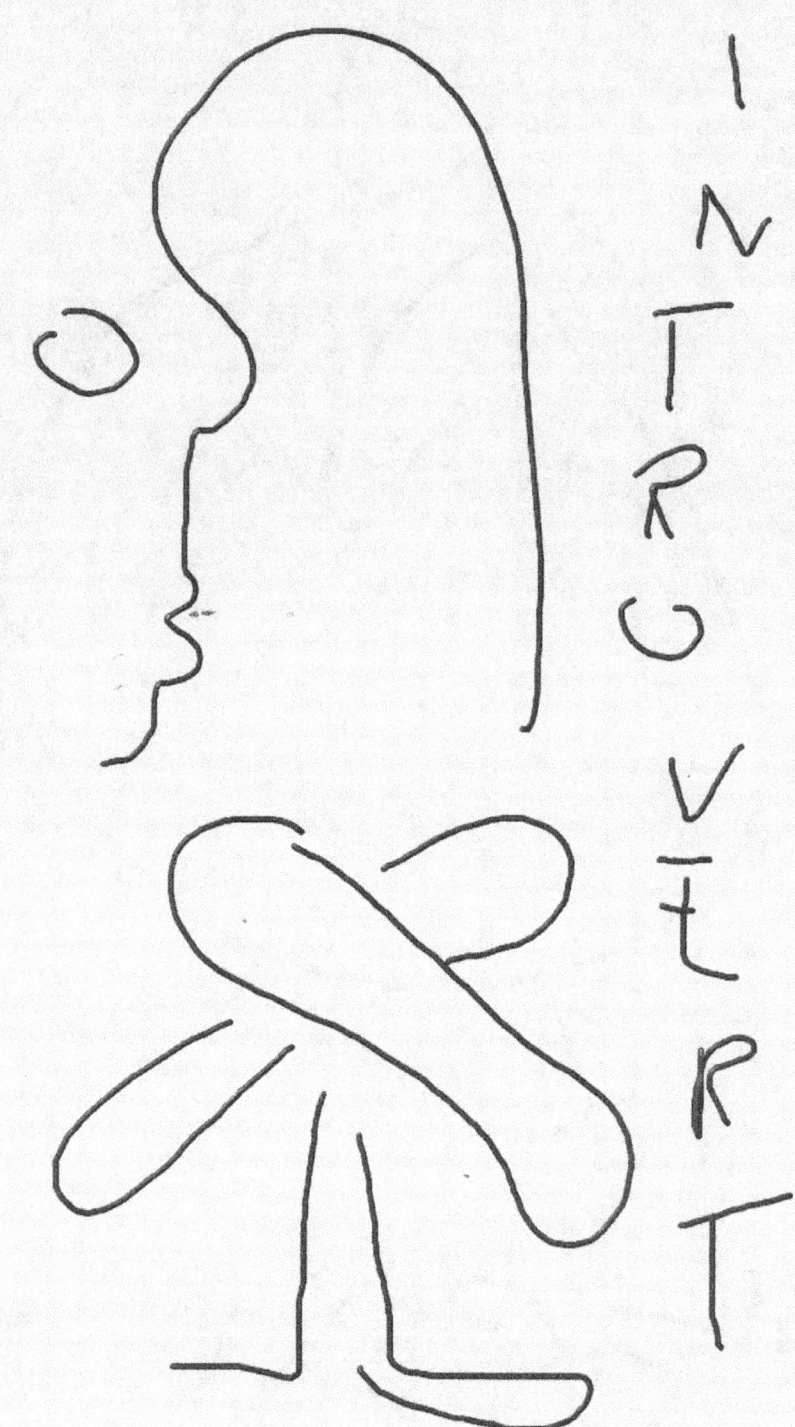

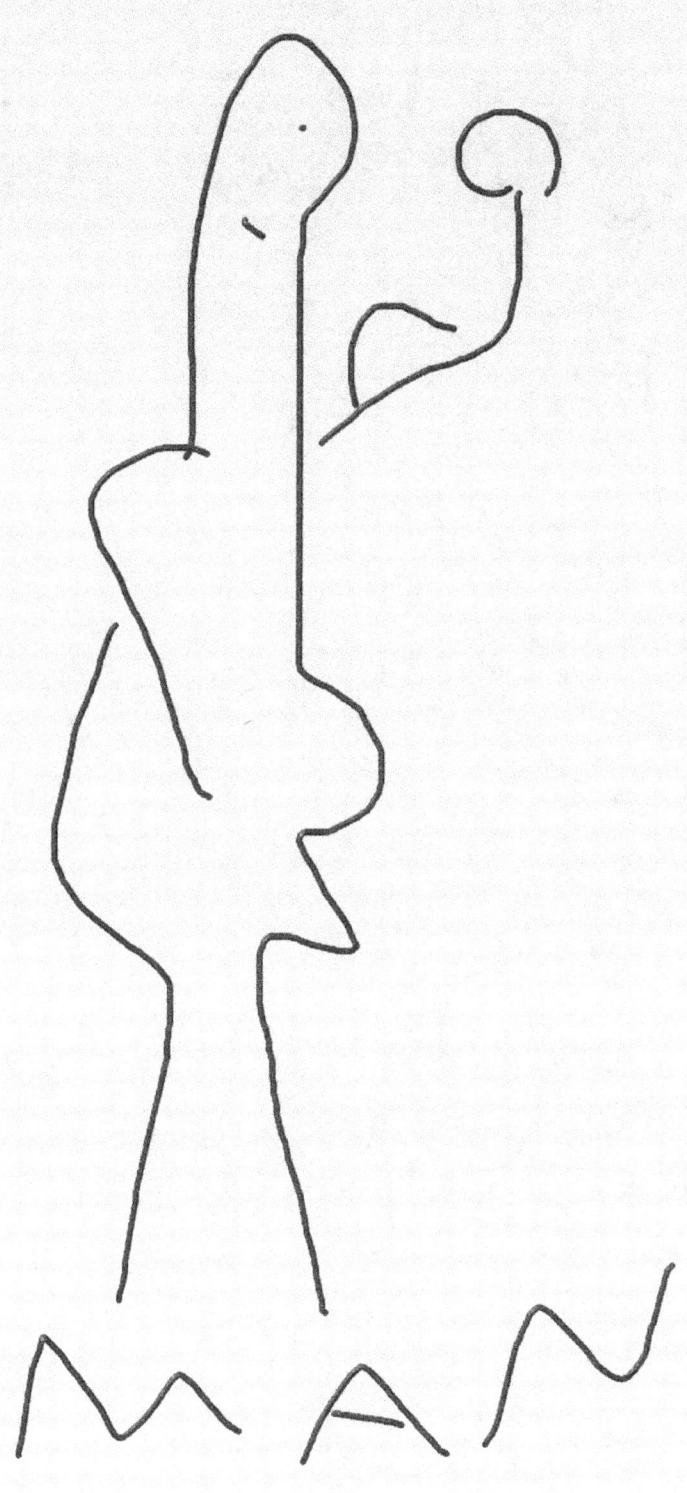

UP IN ARMS

Keyes

10/14/13

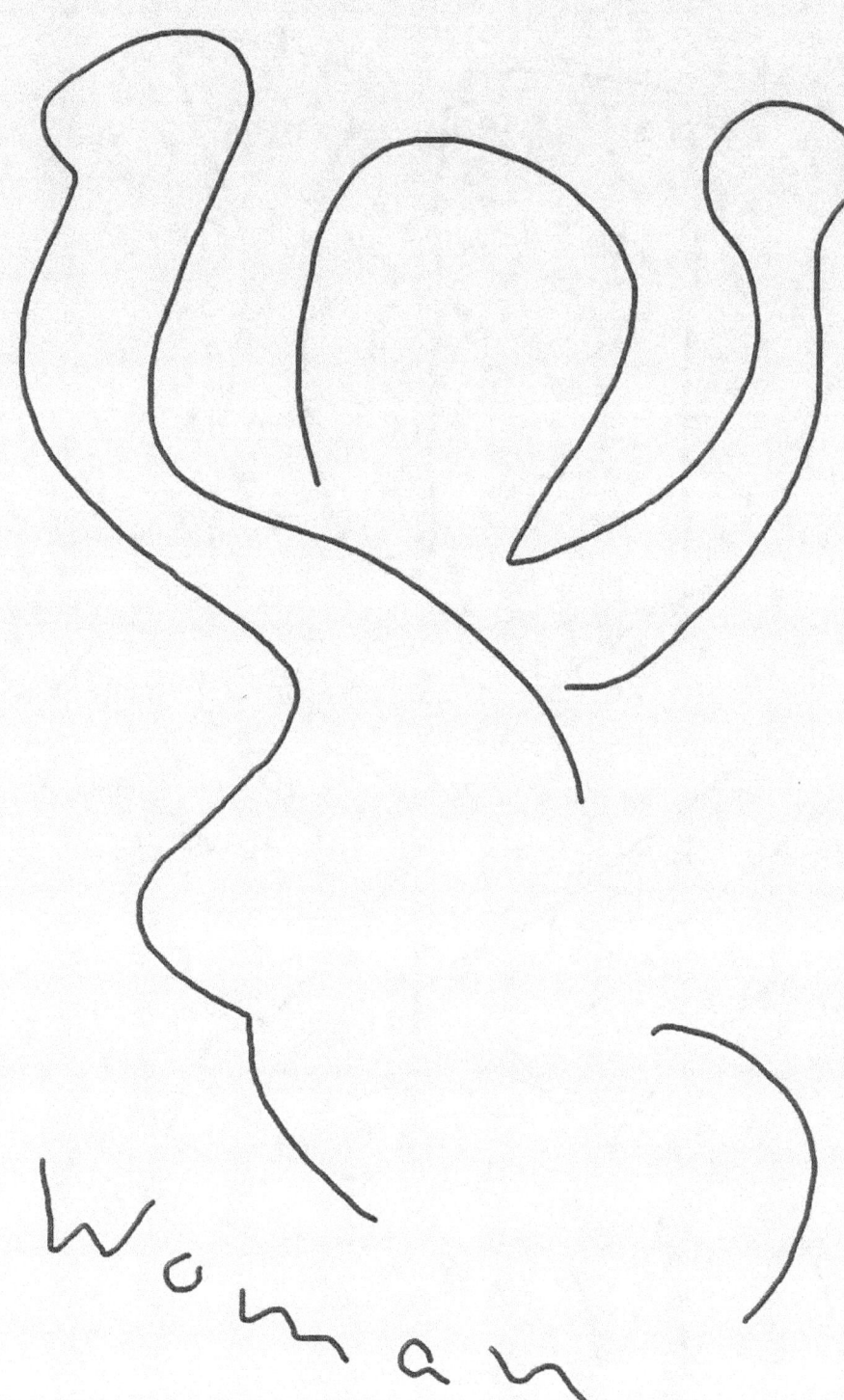

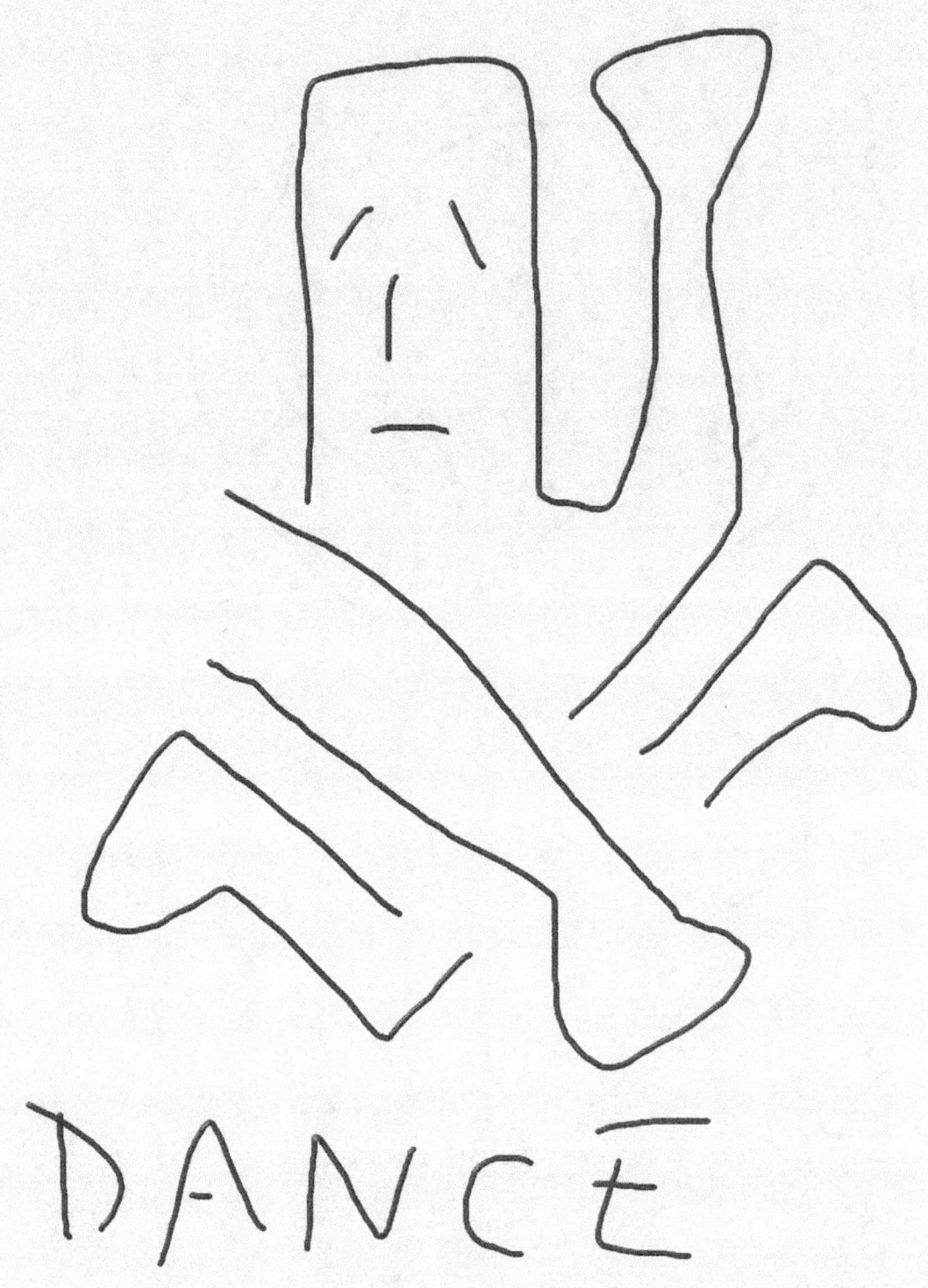

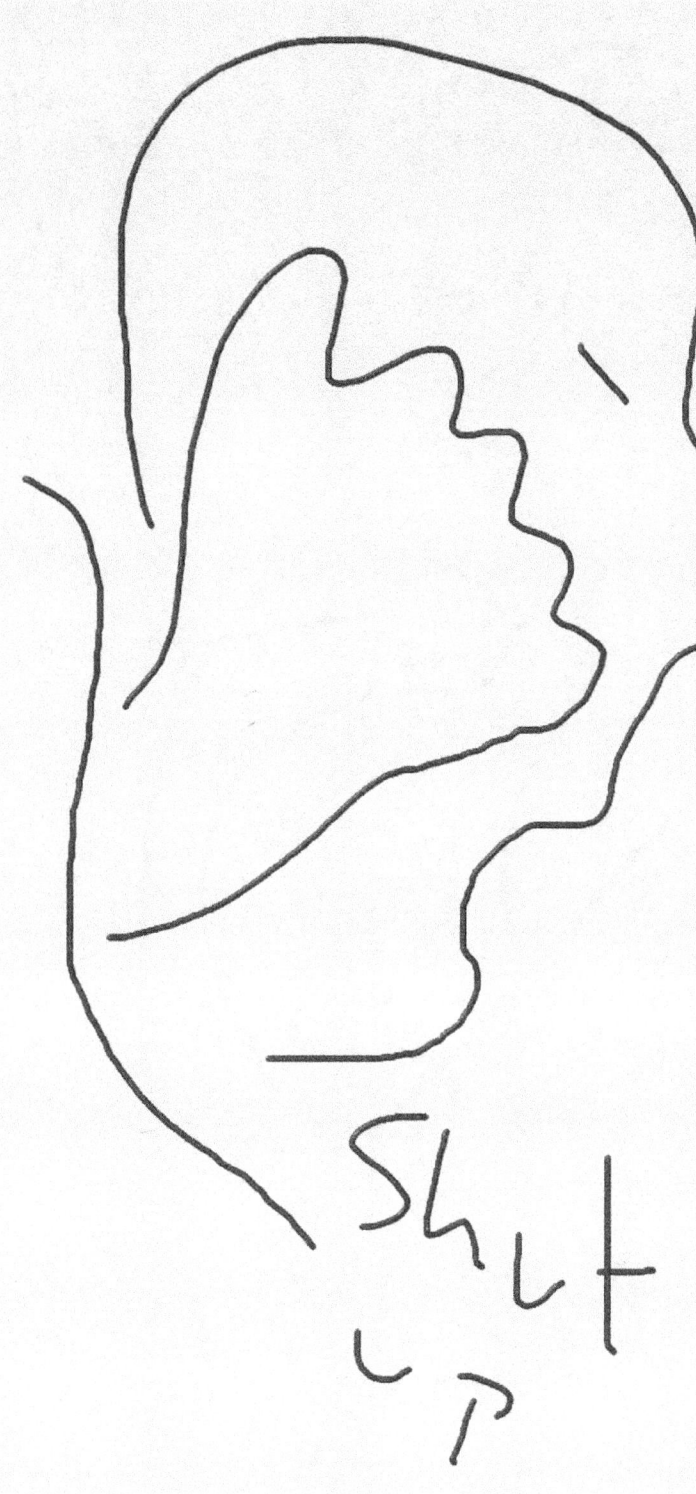

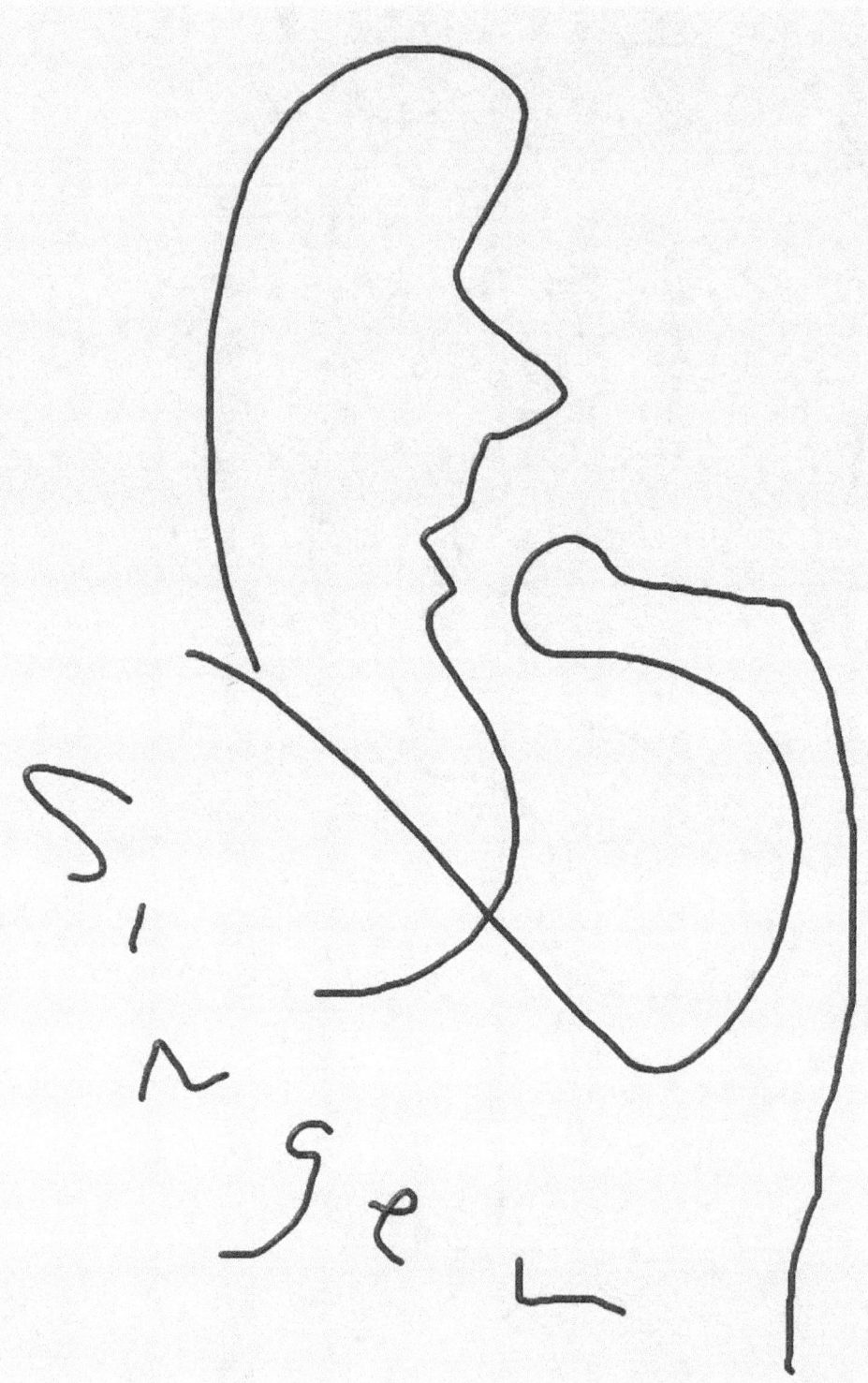

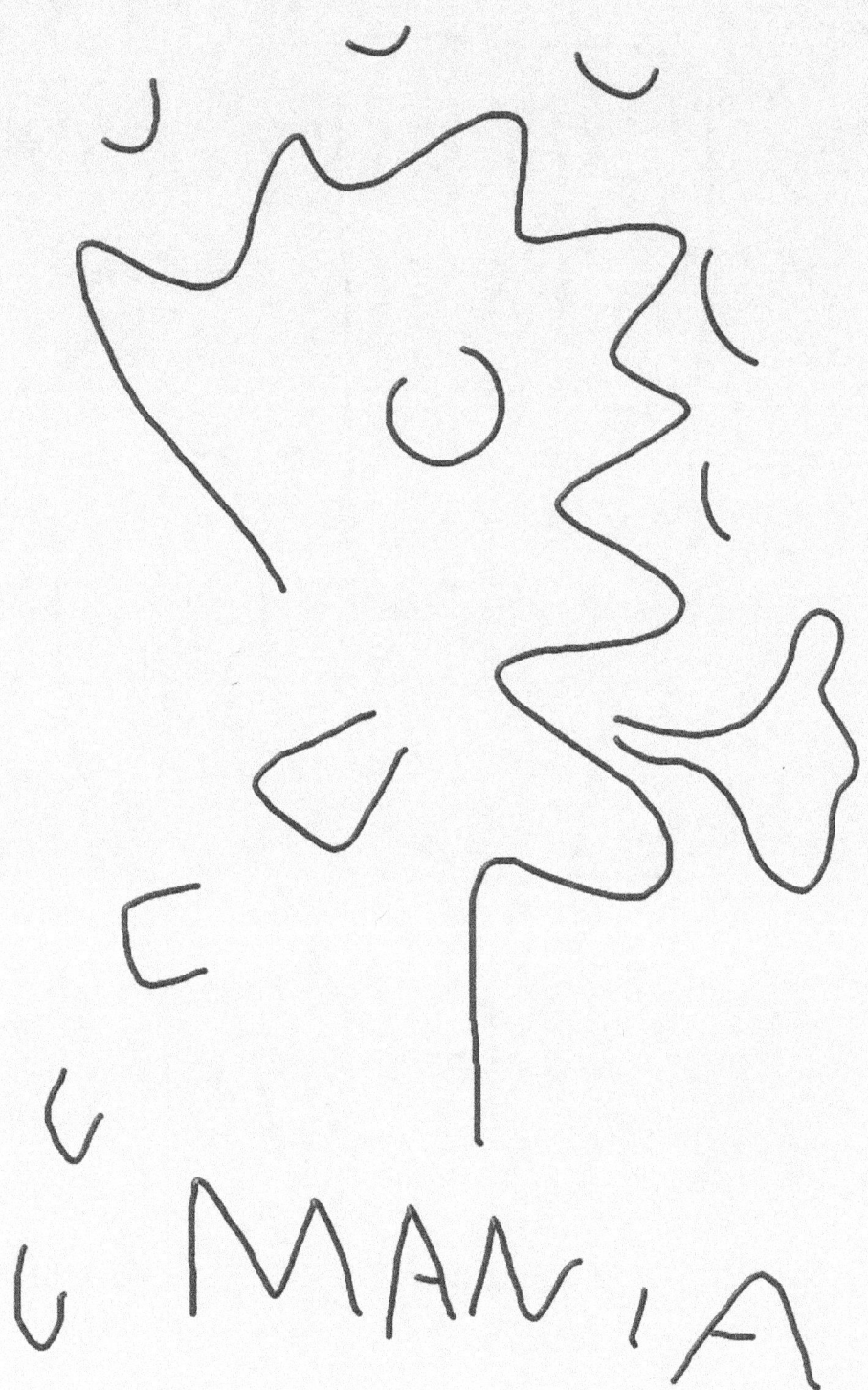

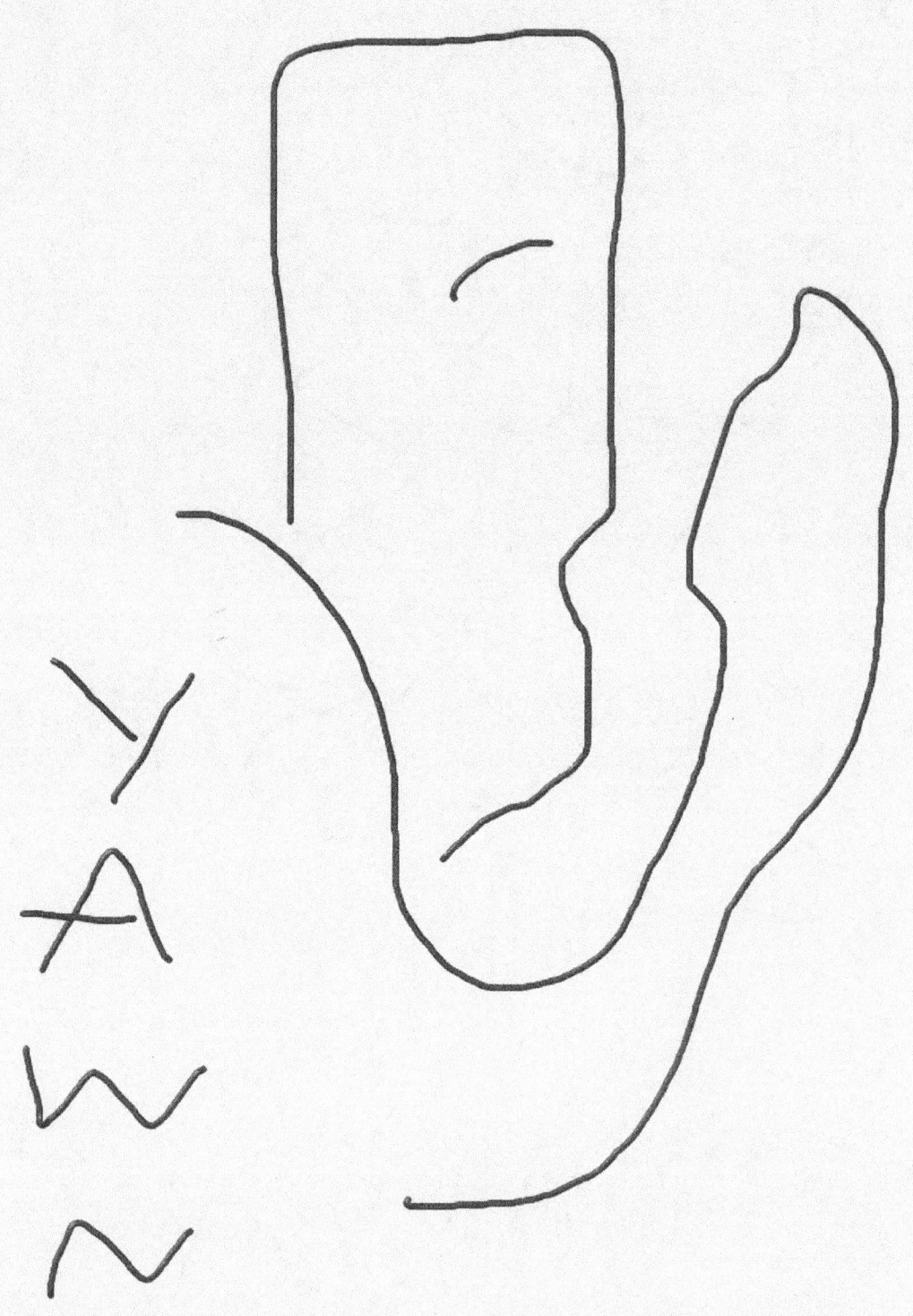

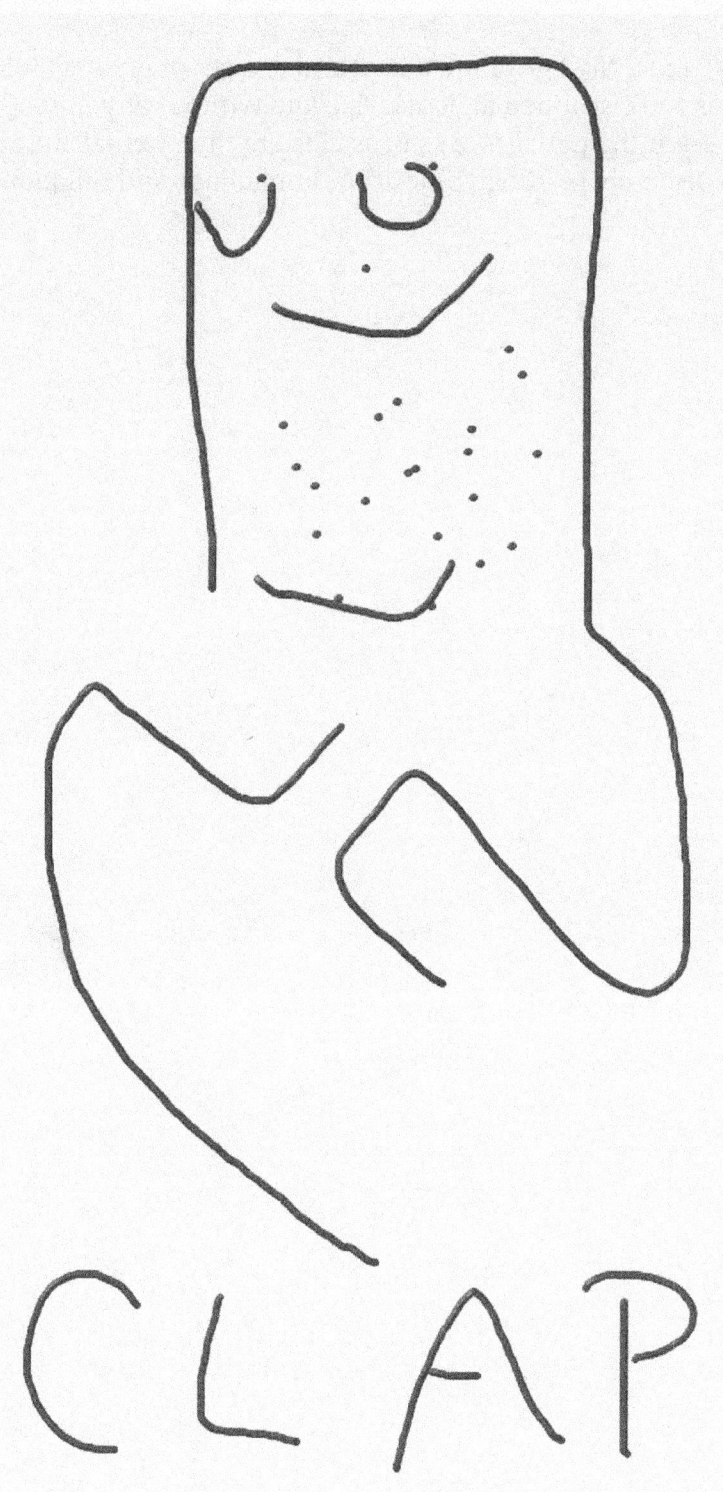

The Pencil Works

Linoglyphs were first recorded using a No.2 graphite pencil and a sheet of plain white copier paper. The oringial images were scanned at actual size and without any photo retouching. The attempt is to present the pencil works in as close to their actual state as possible in accordance with the principle of linoglyphic art of immediacy and uniqueness.

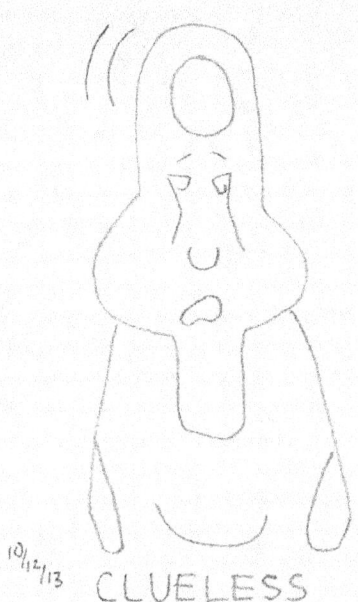

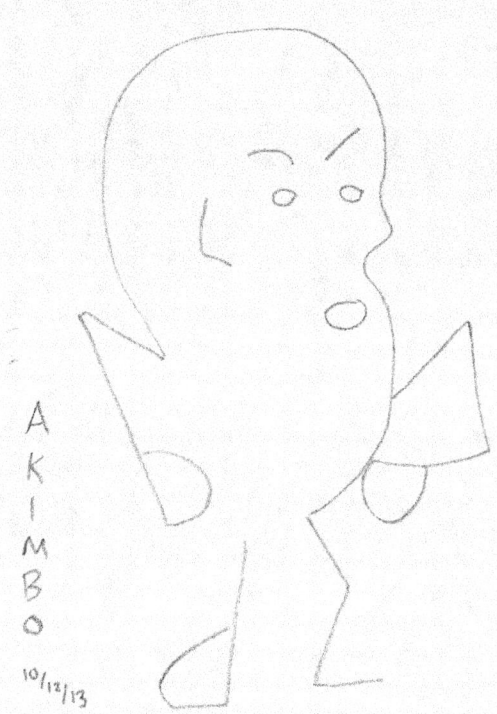

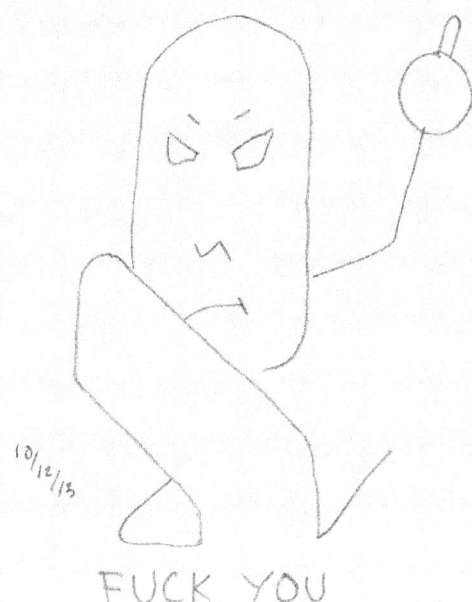

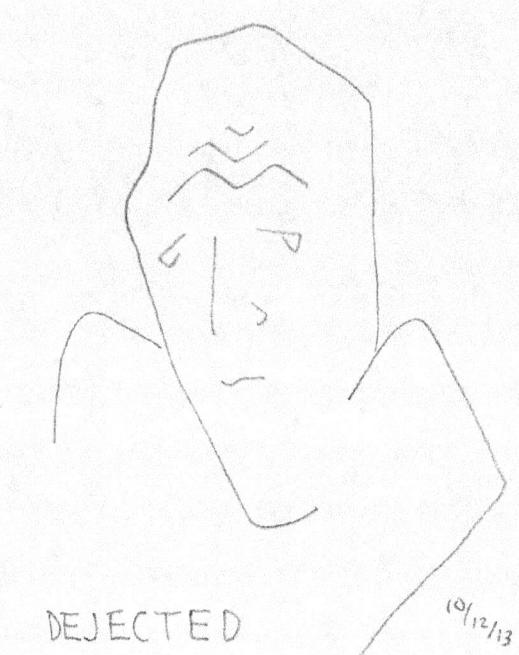

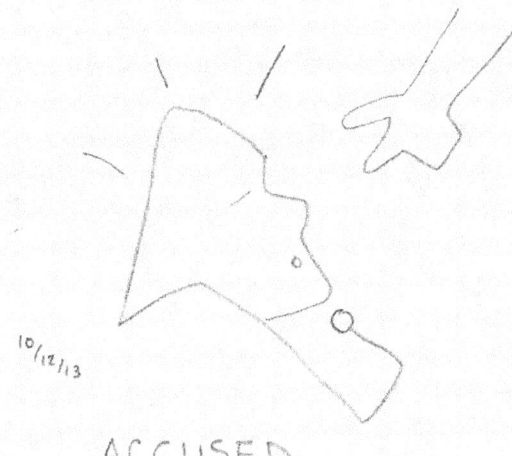
ACCUSED

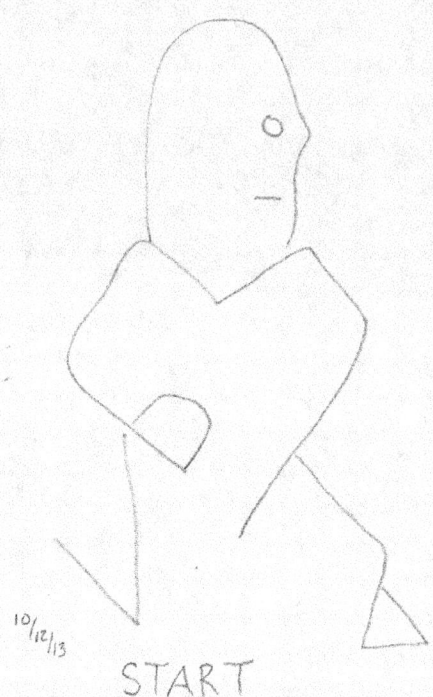
START

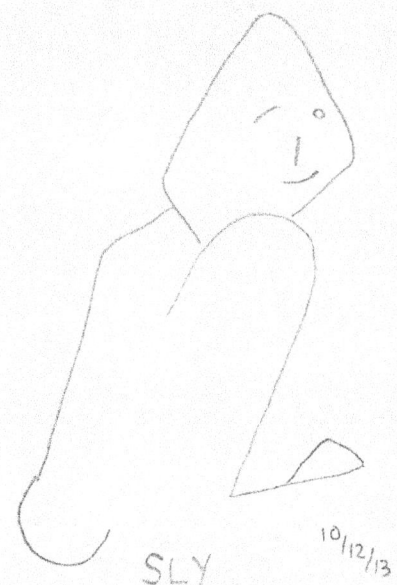

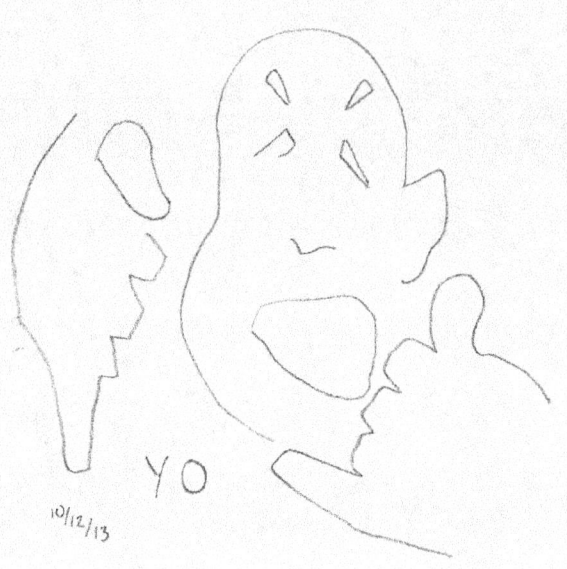

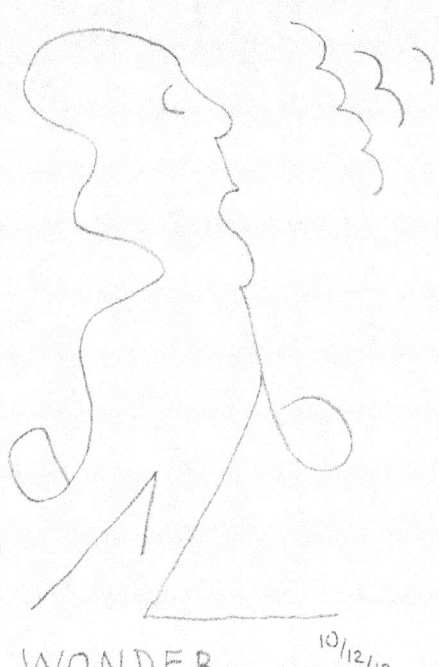

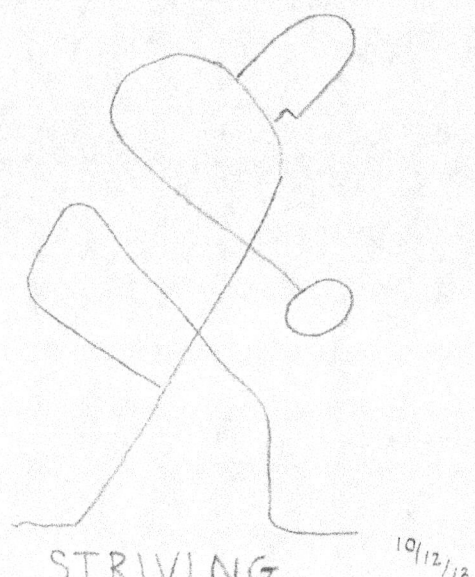

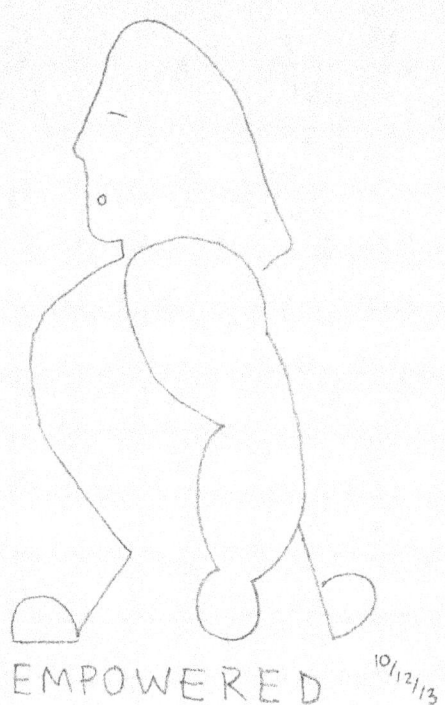

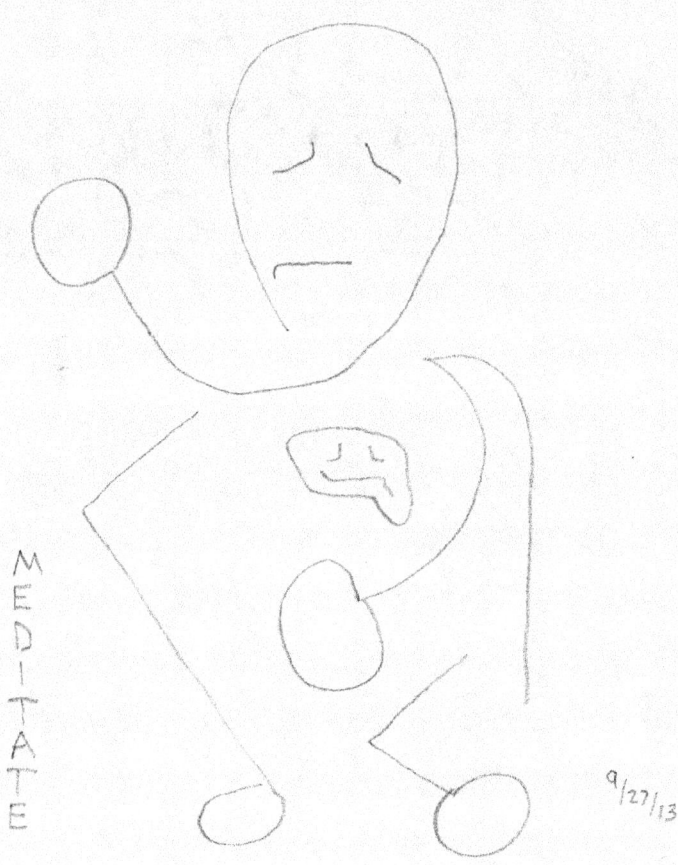

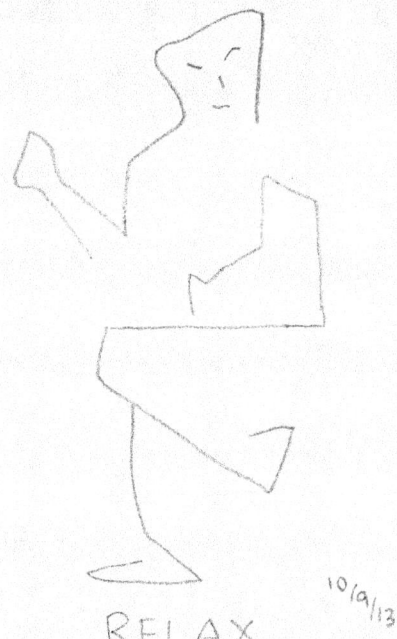

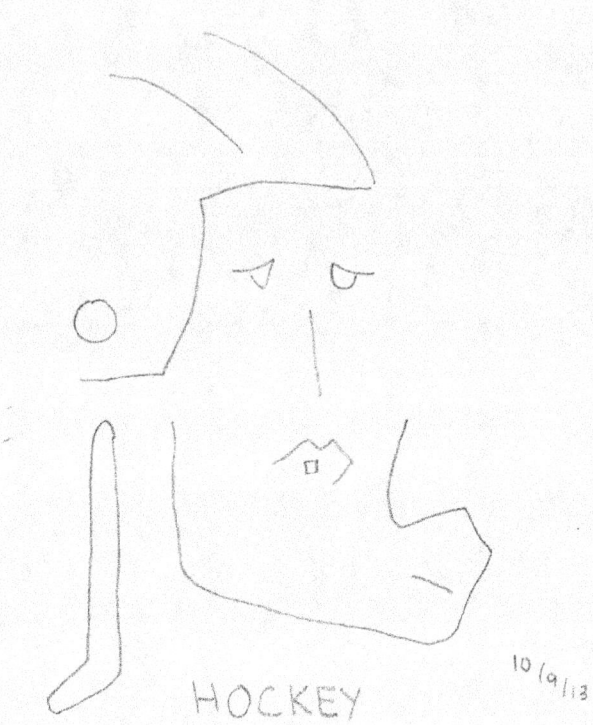

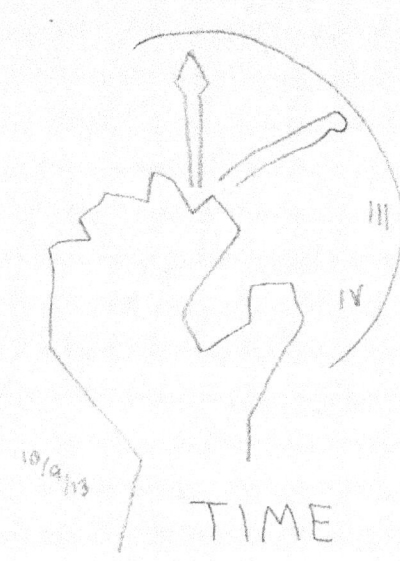

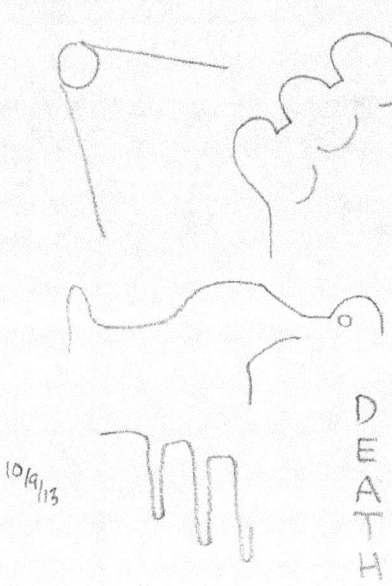

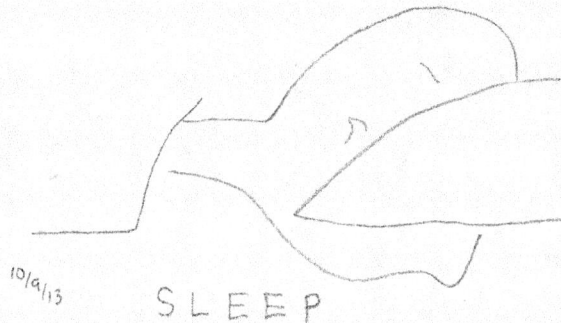

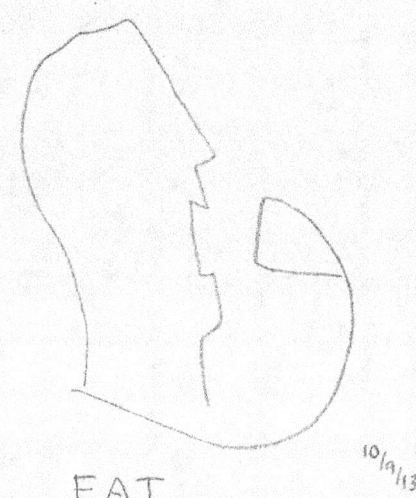

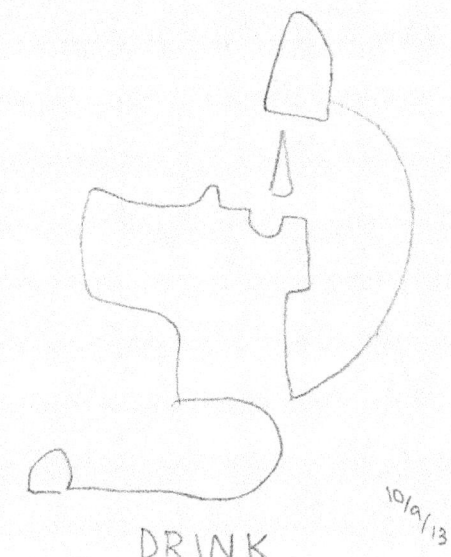

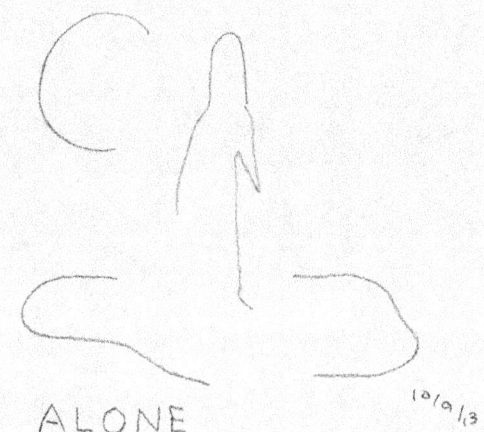

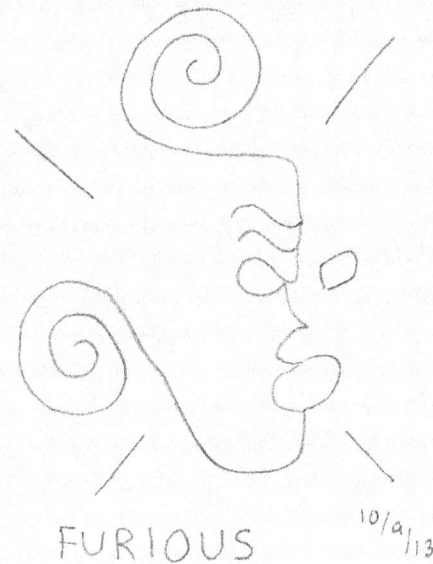

FURIOUS 10/9/13

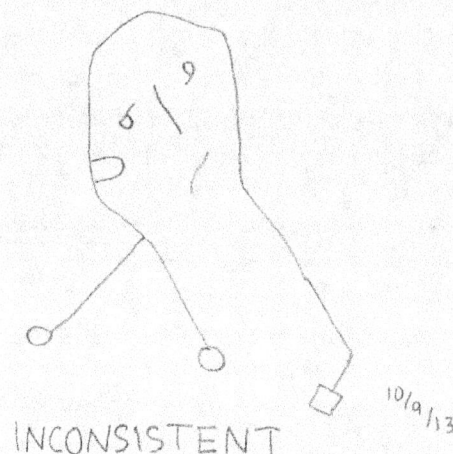

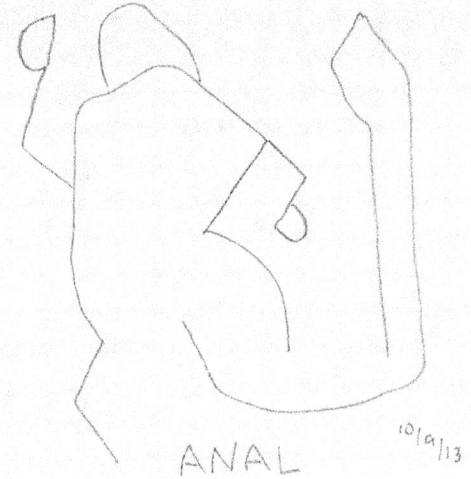

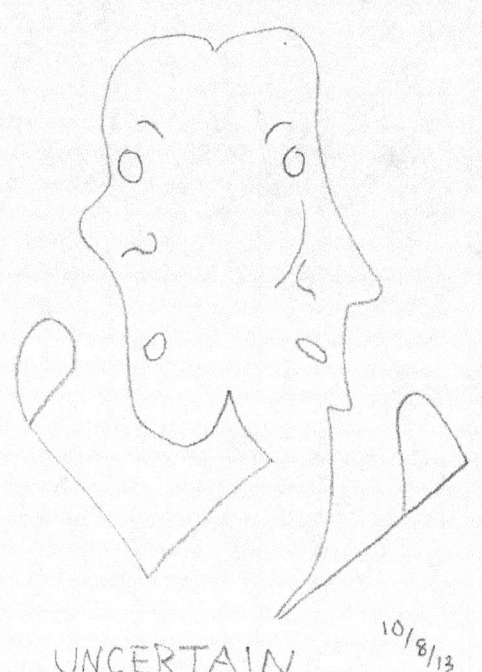

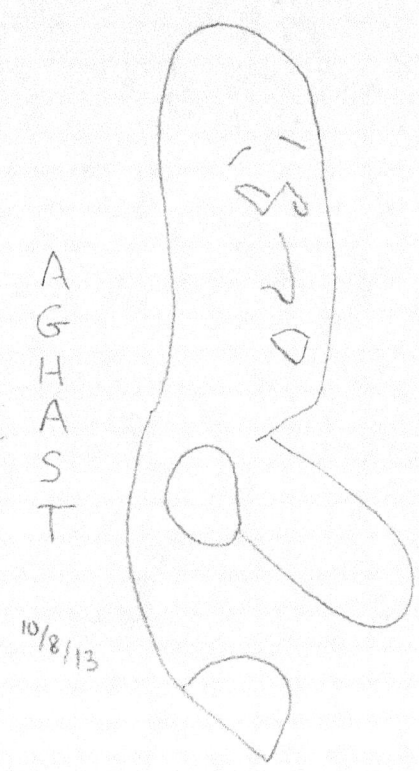

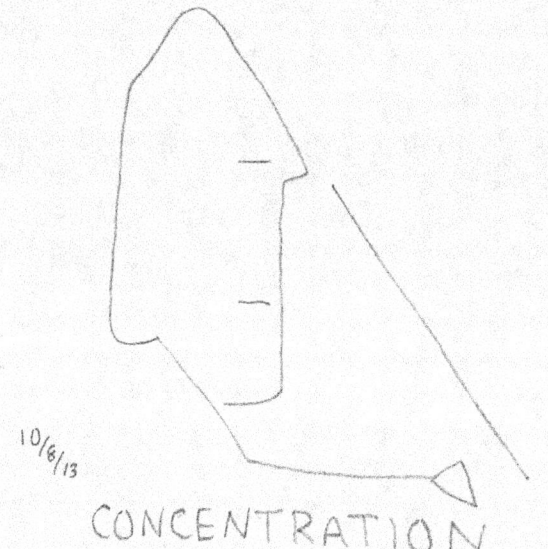

CONCENTRATION

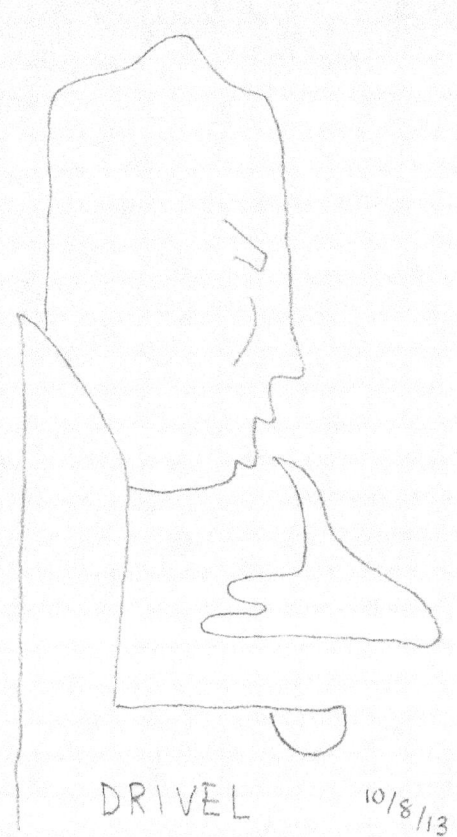

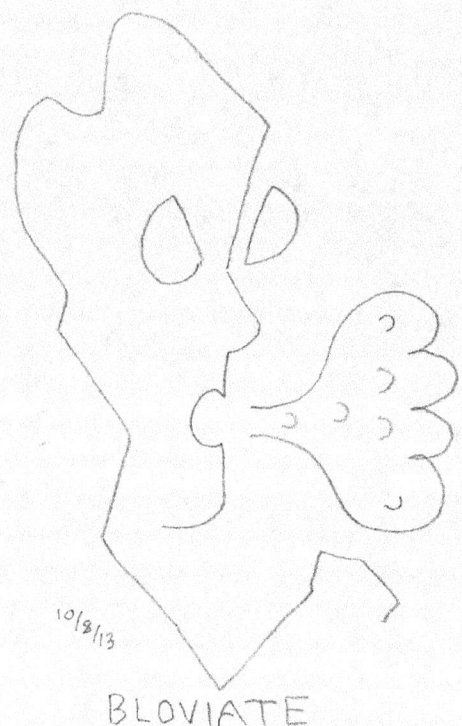

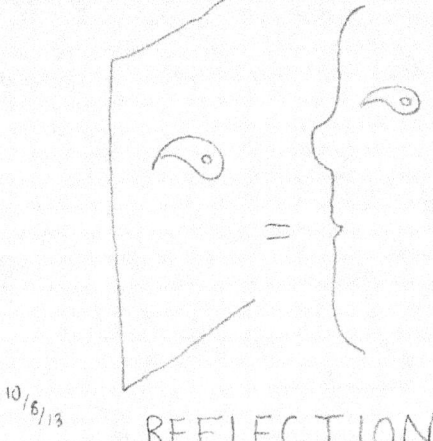

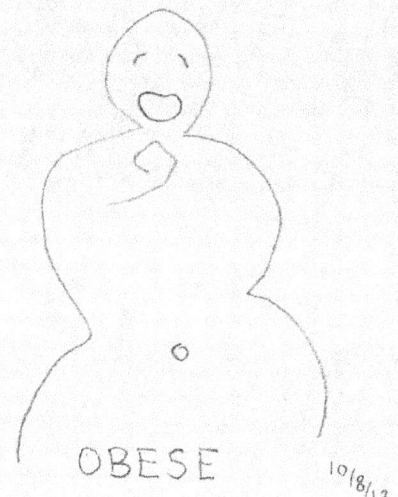

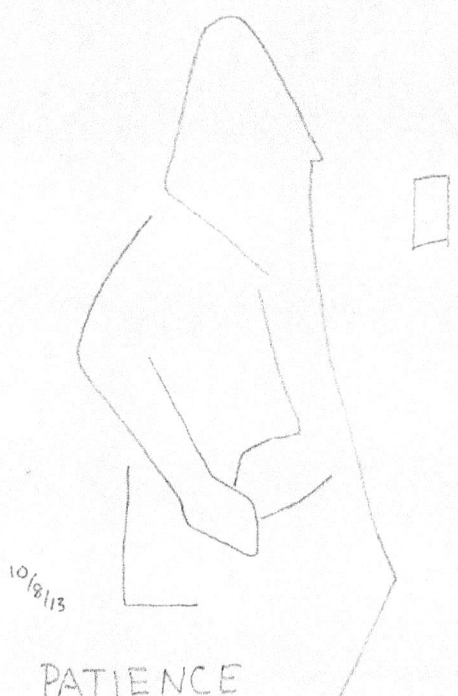

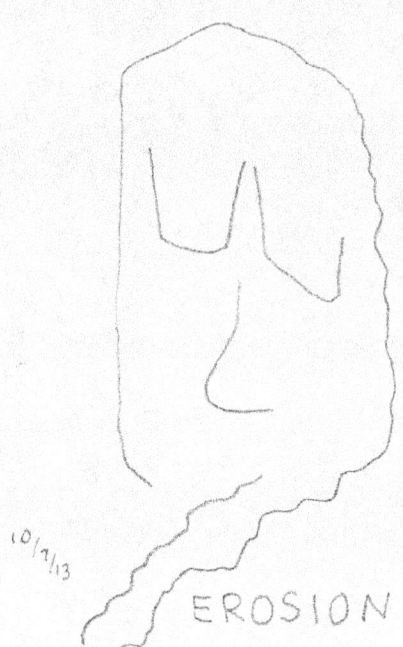

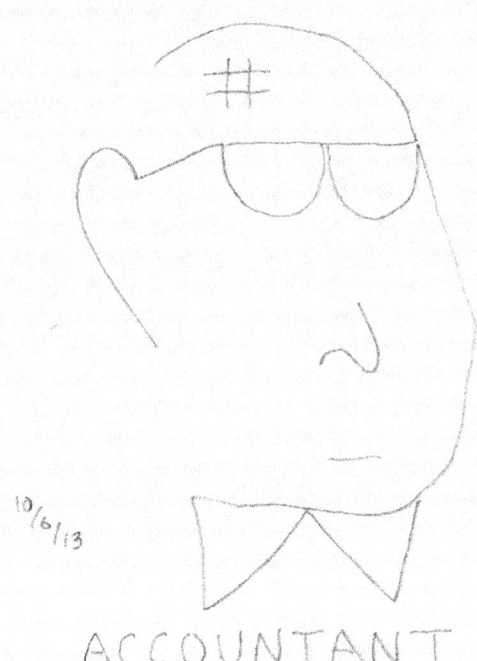

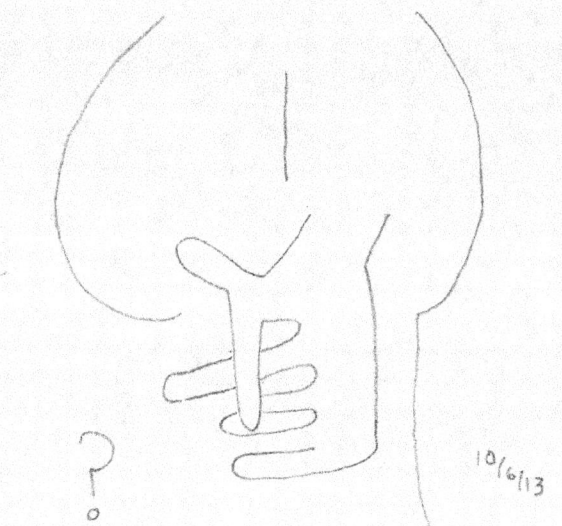

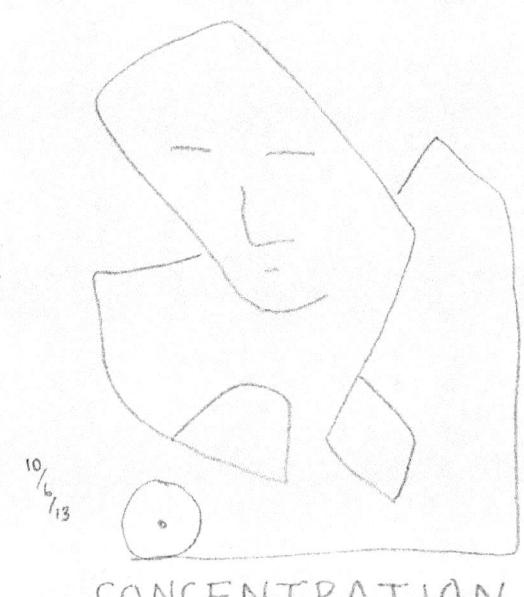

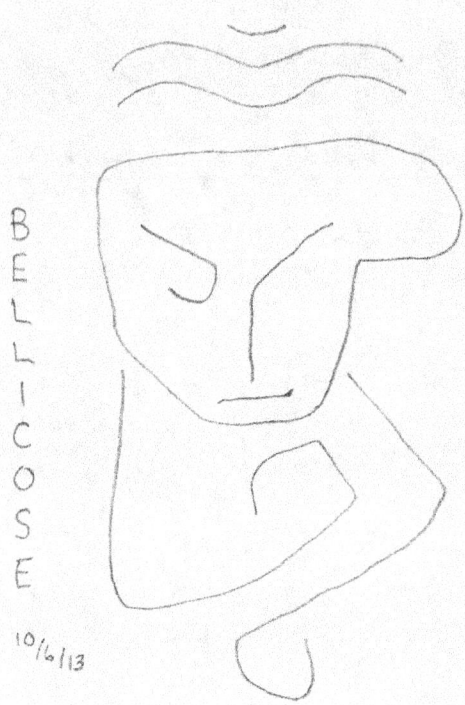

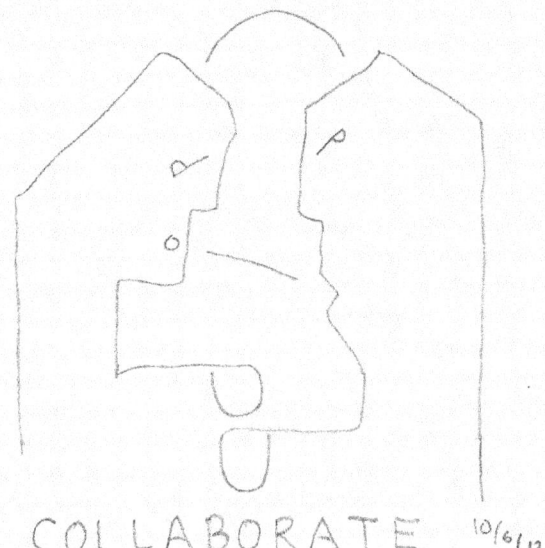
COLLABORATE 10/6/13

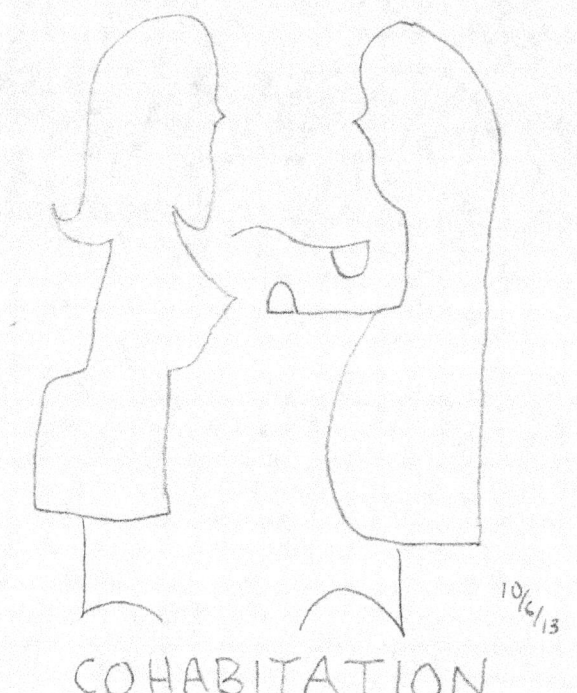

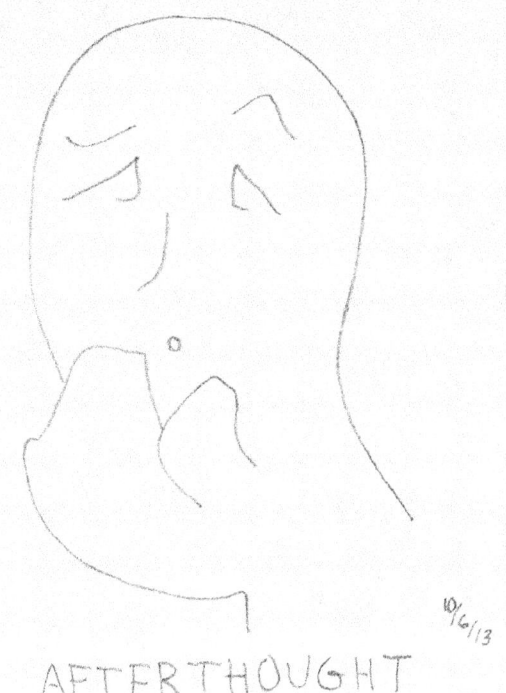

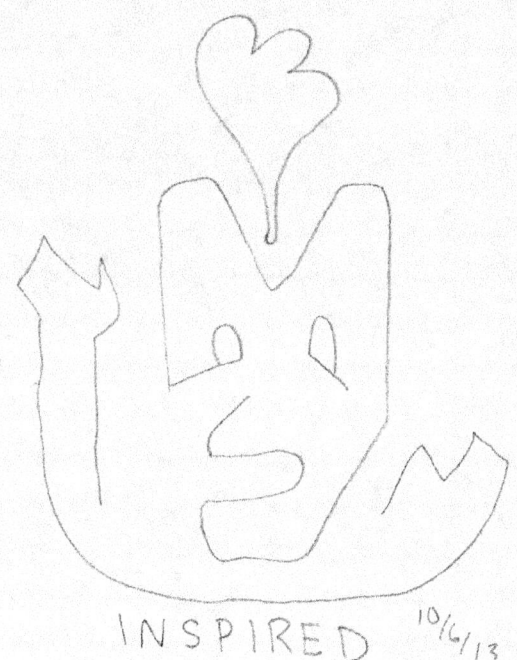

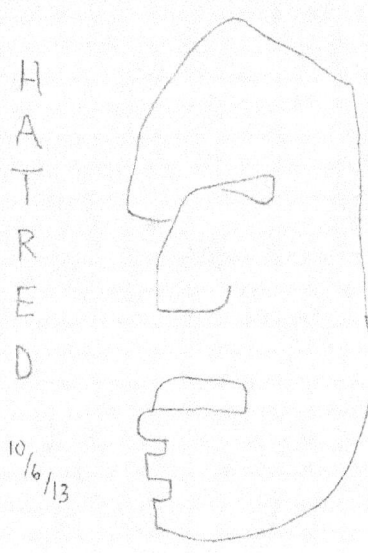

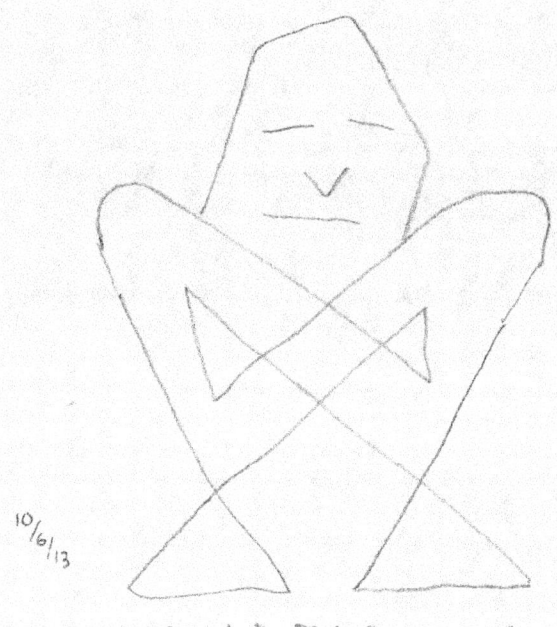

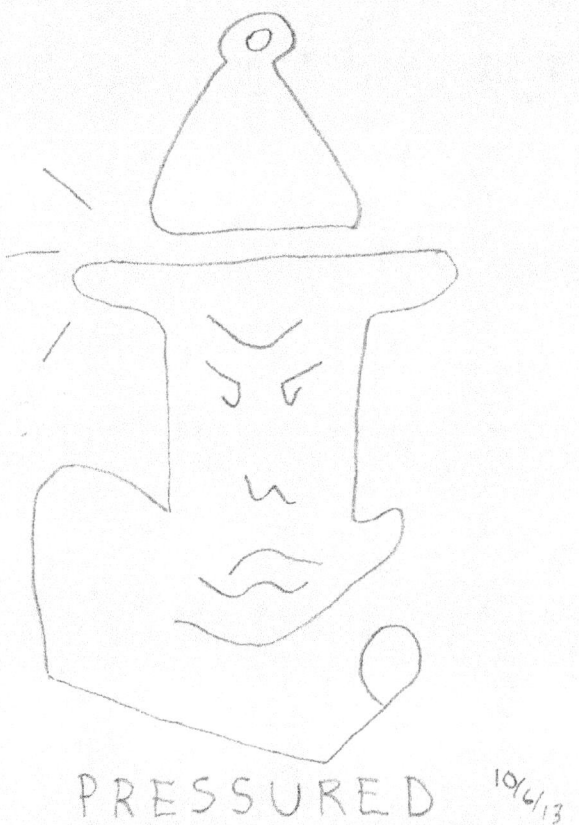

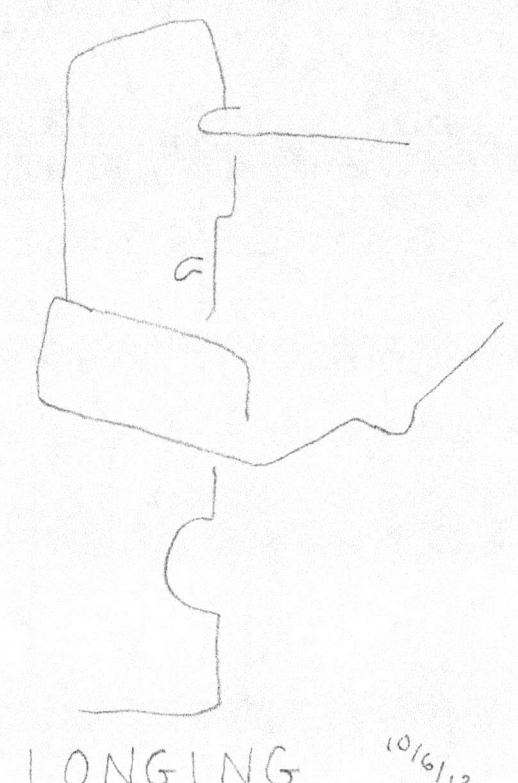

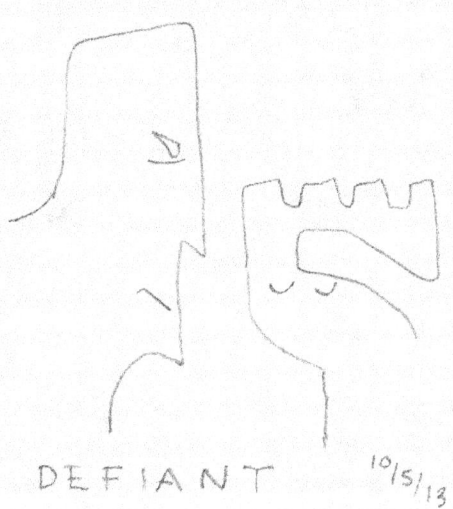

HARDSHIP   10/5/13

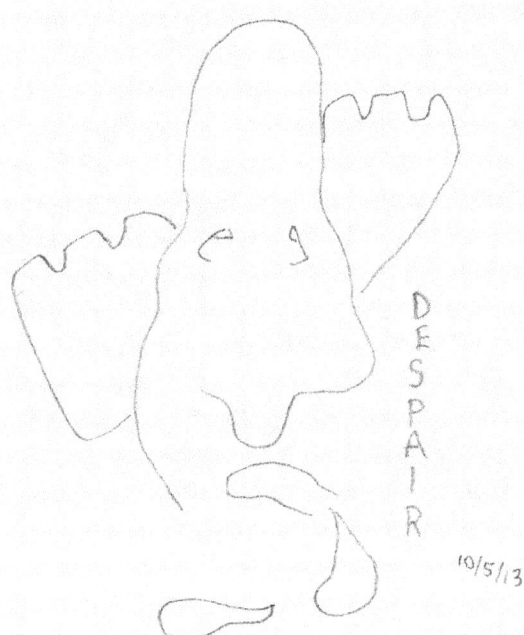

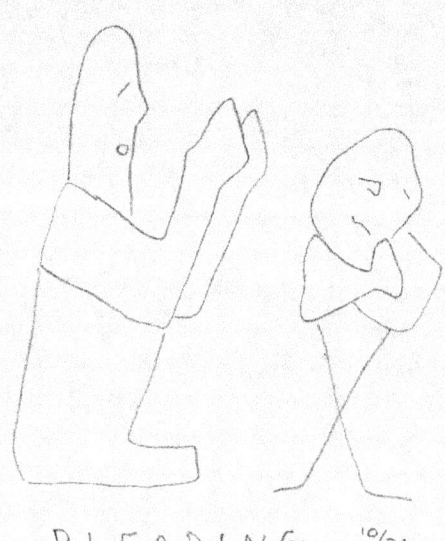

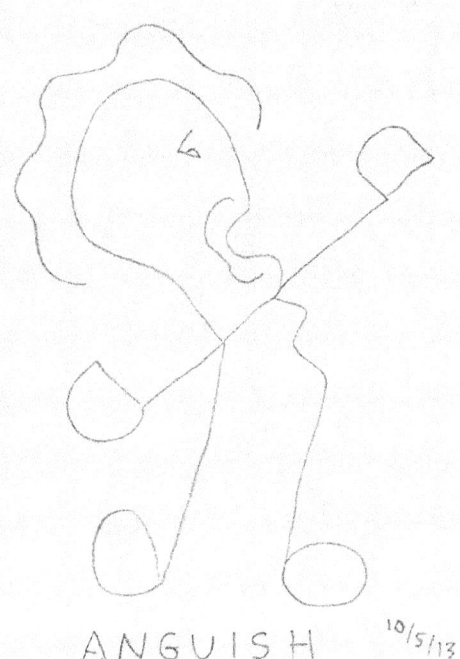

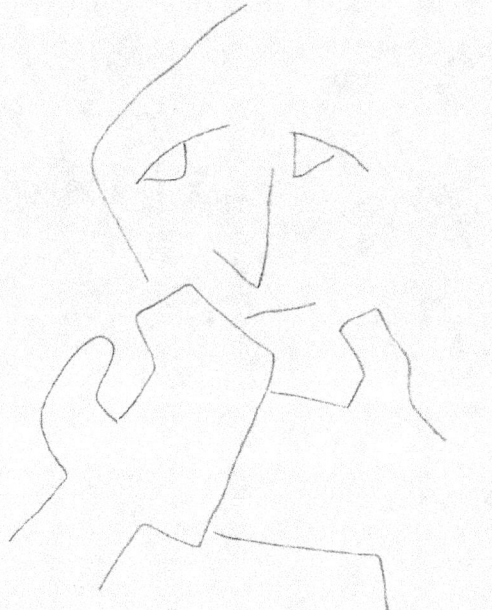

SELF-AWARENESS 10/4/13

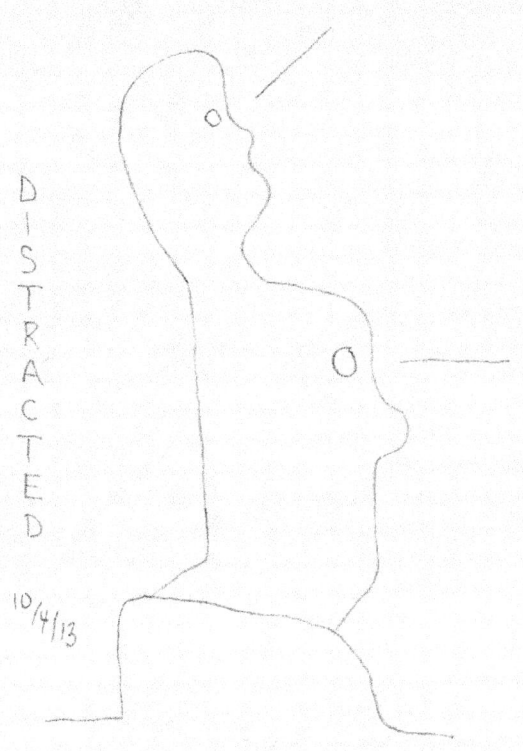

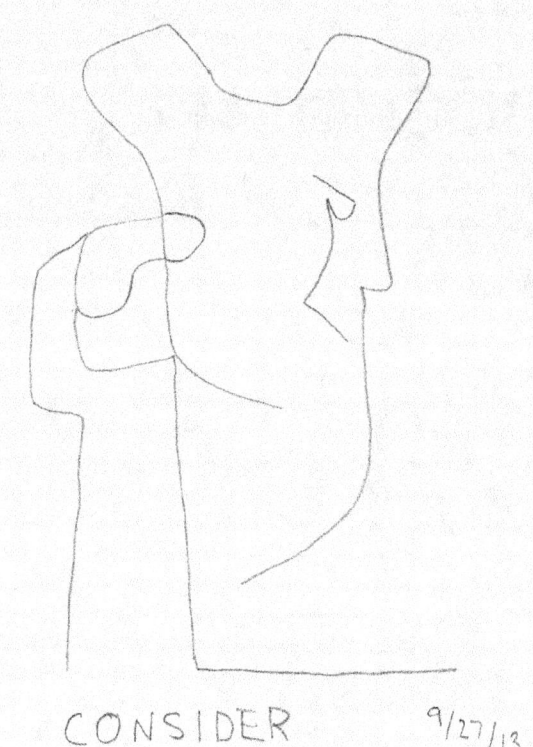

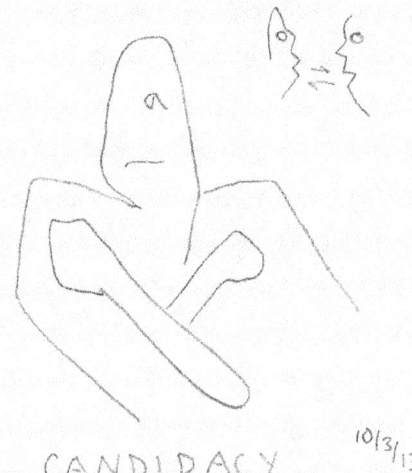

CANDIDACY 10/3/13

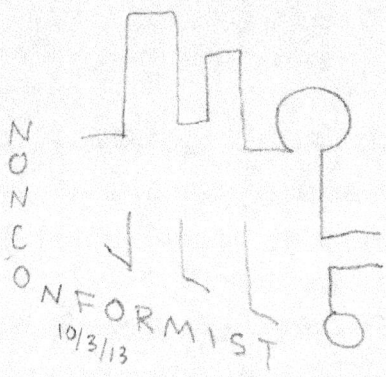

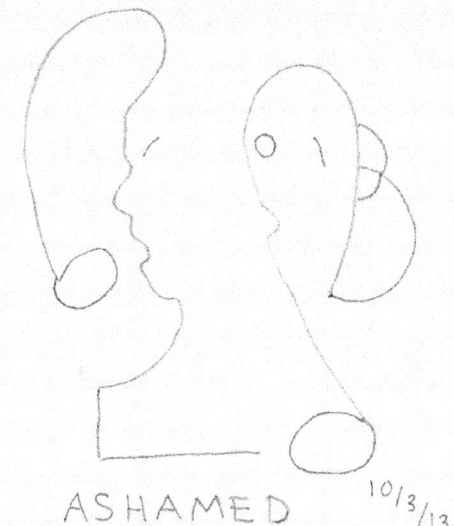

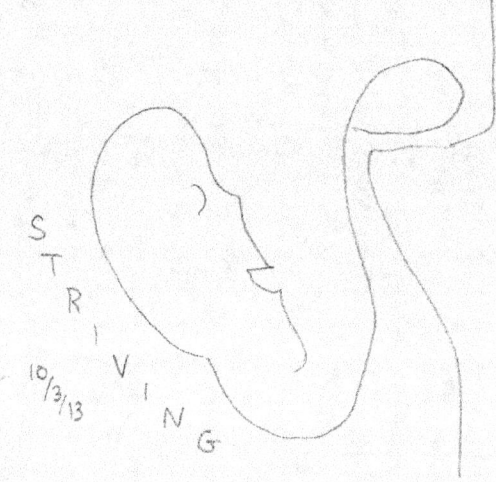

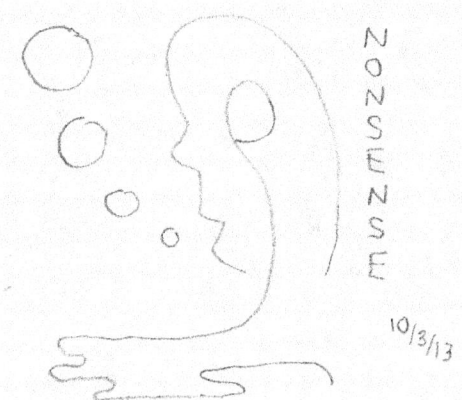

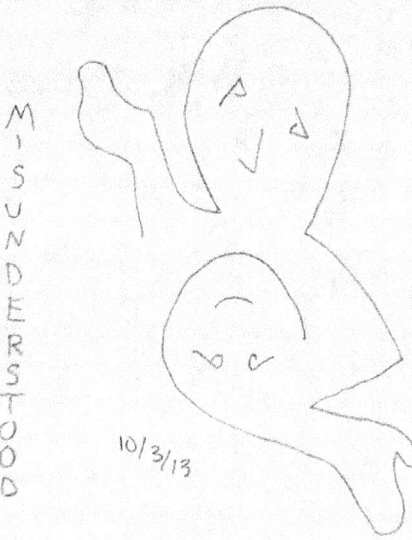

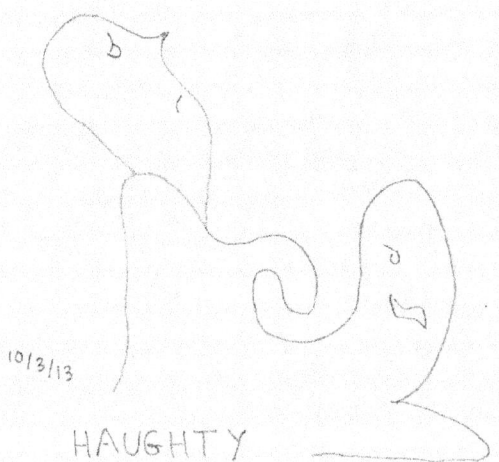

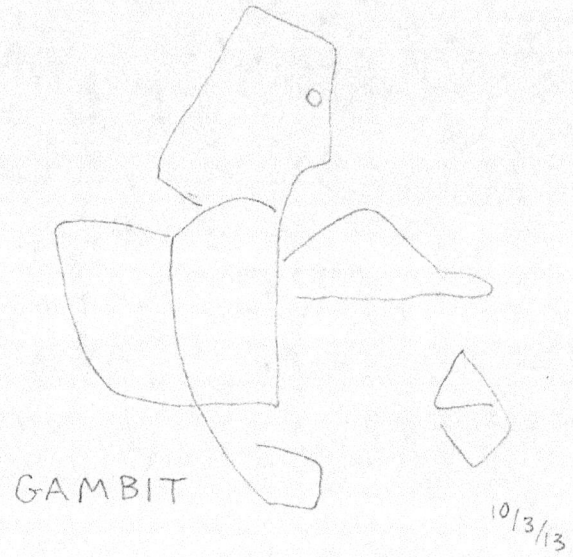

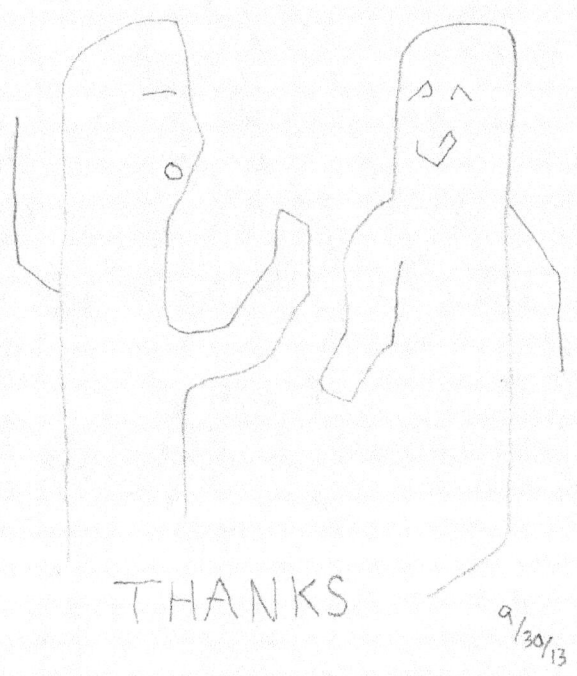

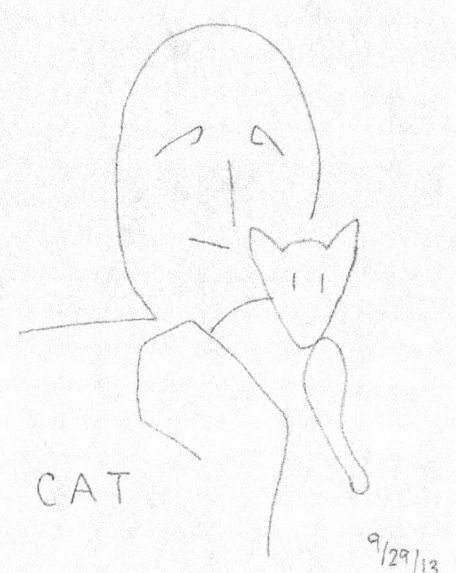

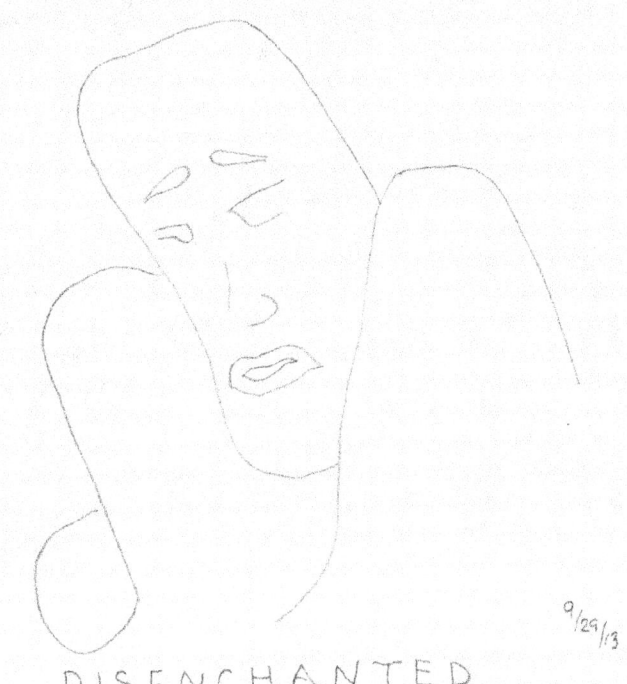

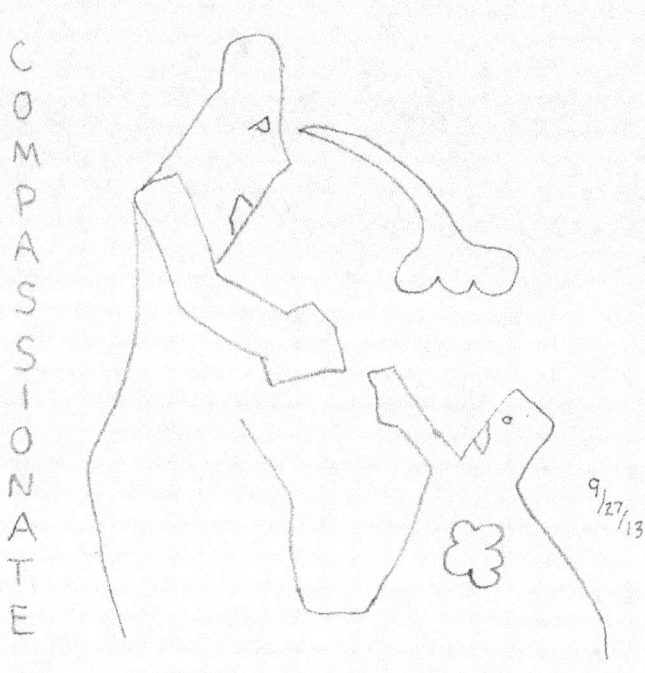

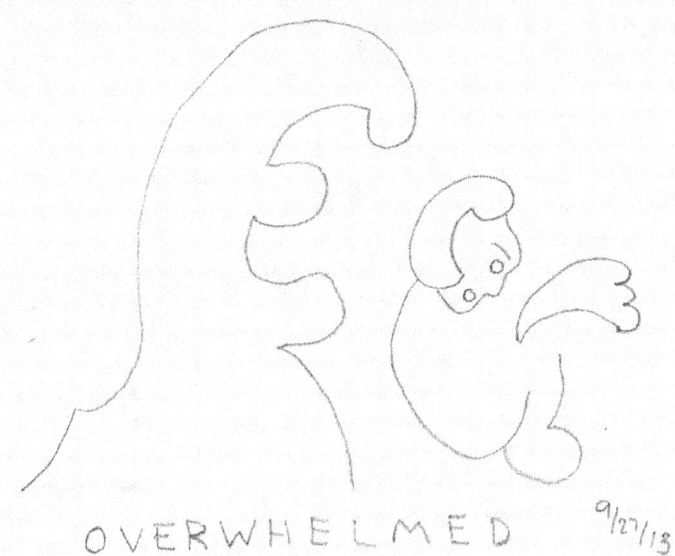

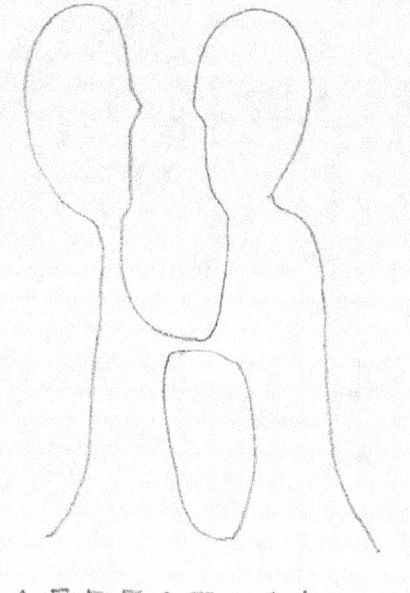

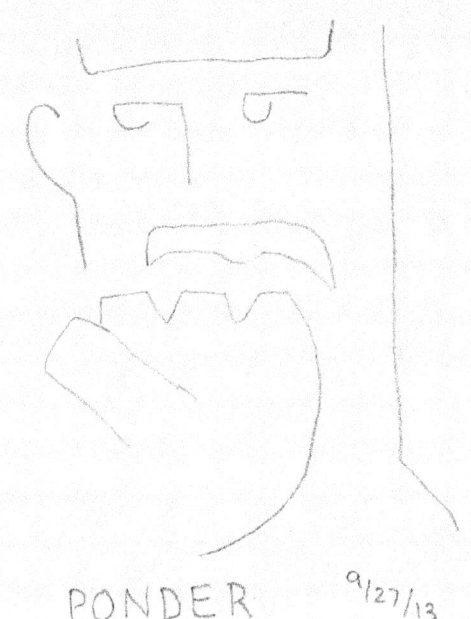

PONDER 9/27/13

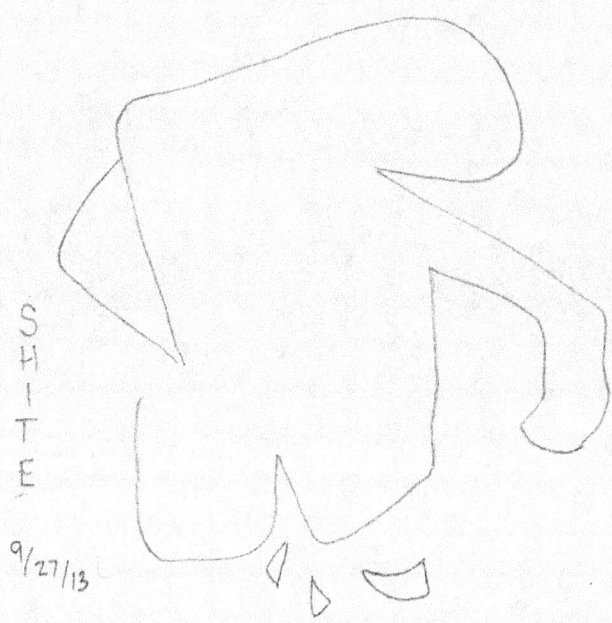

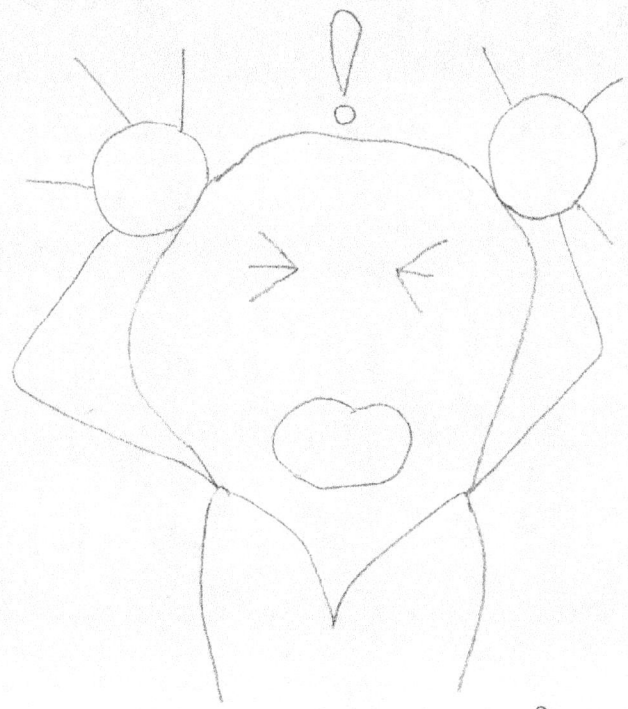

FRUSTRATION 9/26/13

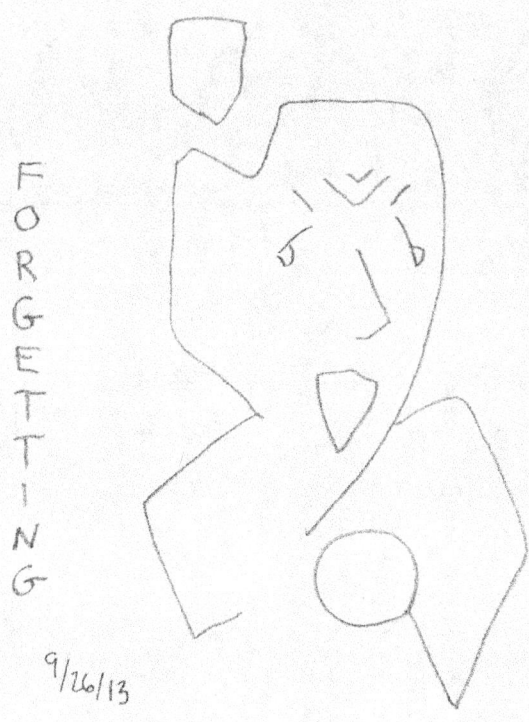

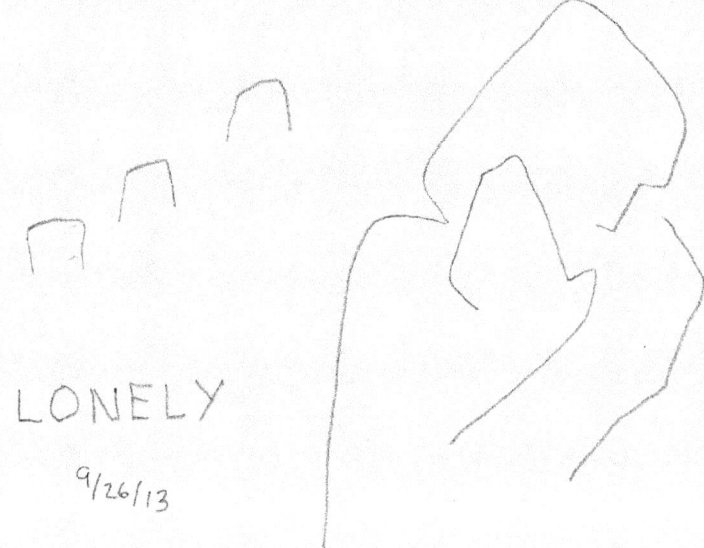

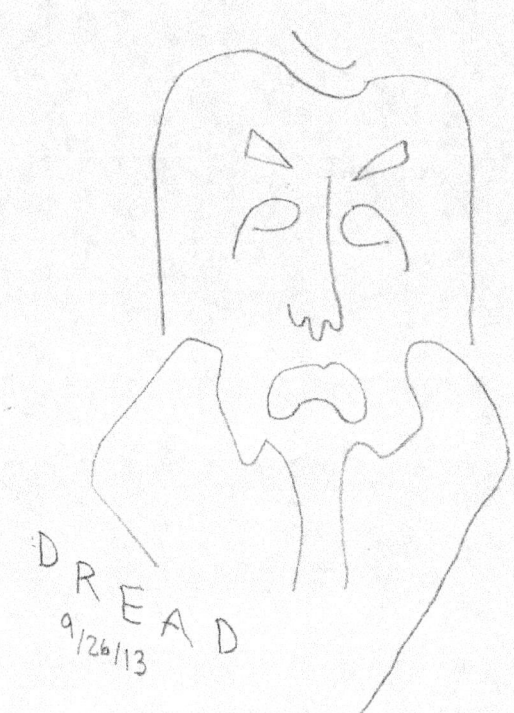

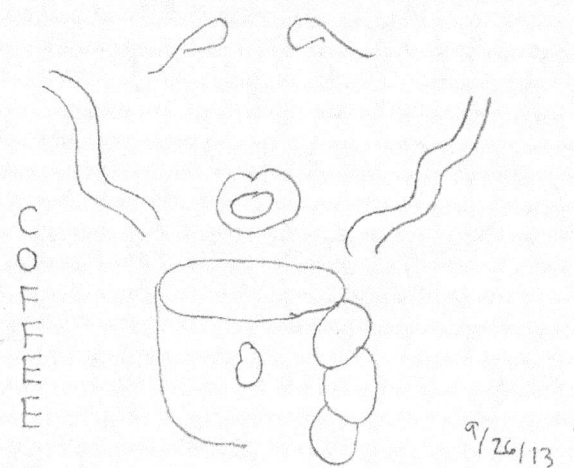

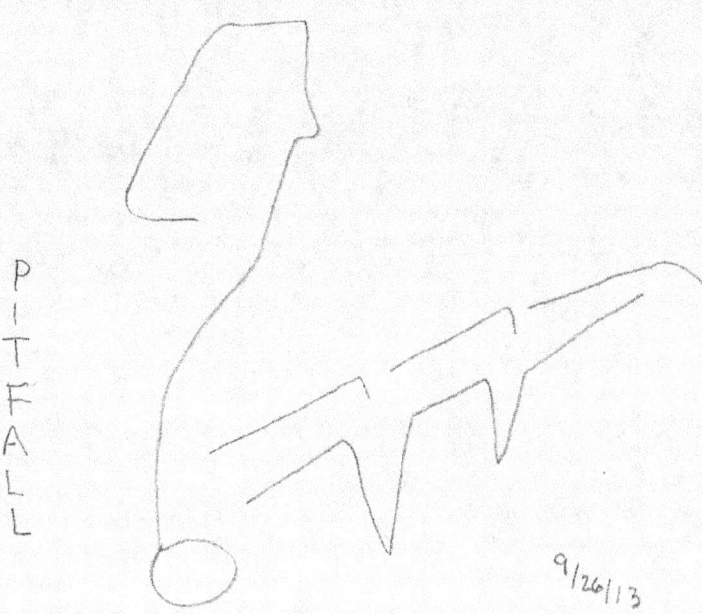

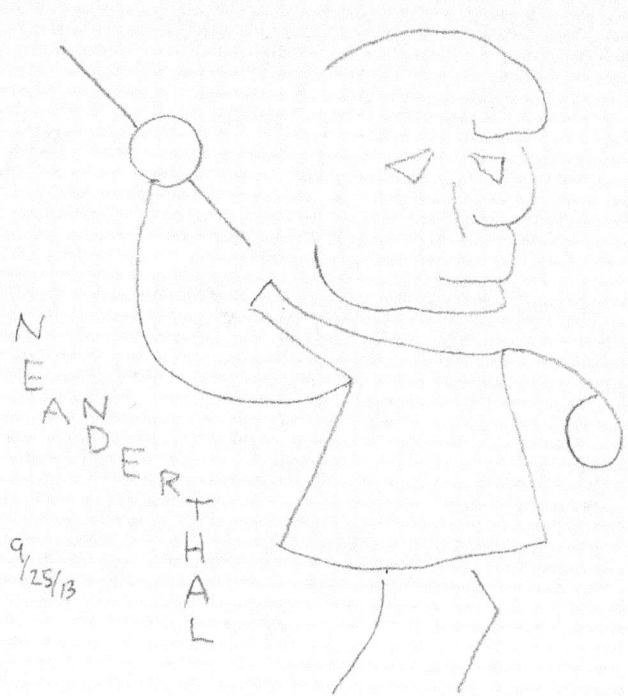

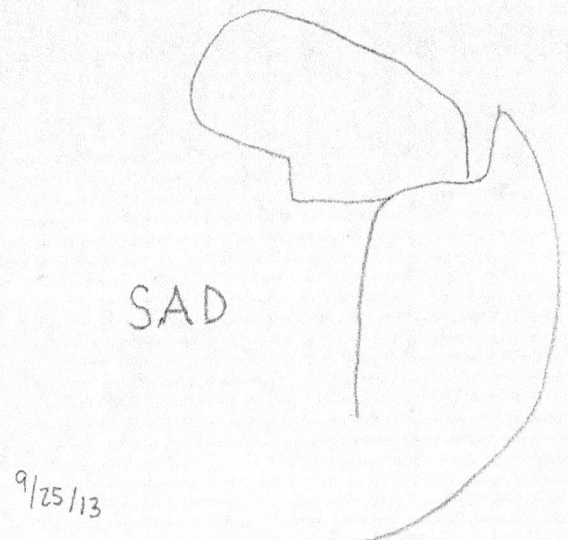

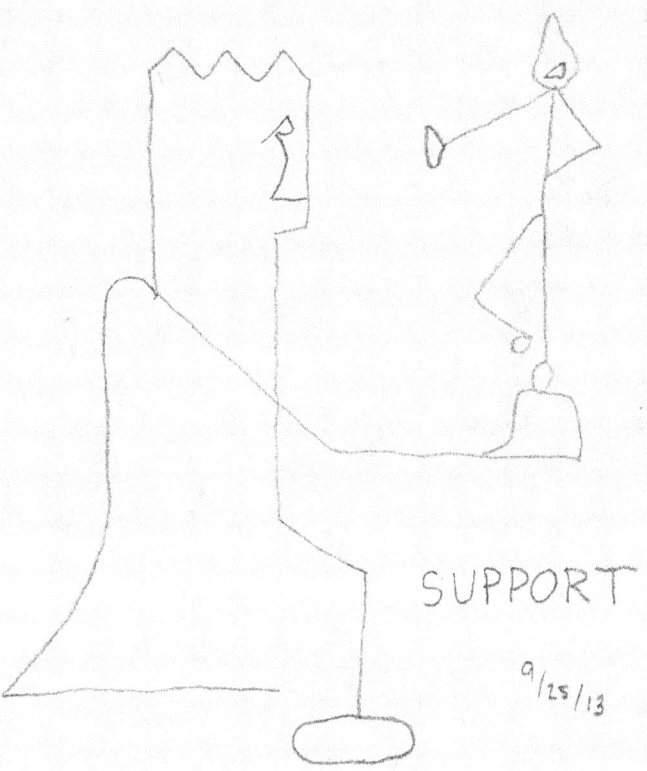

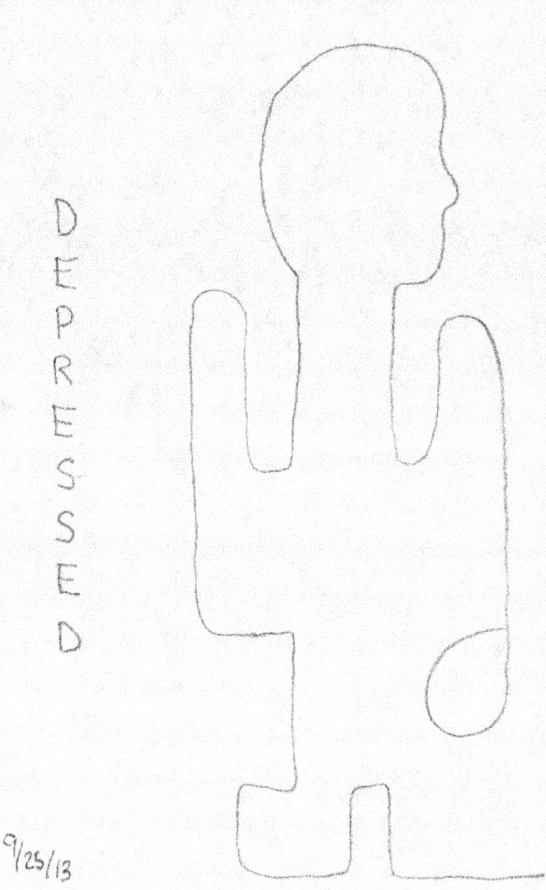

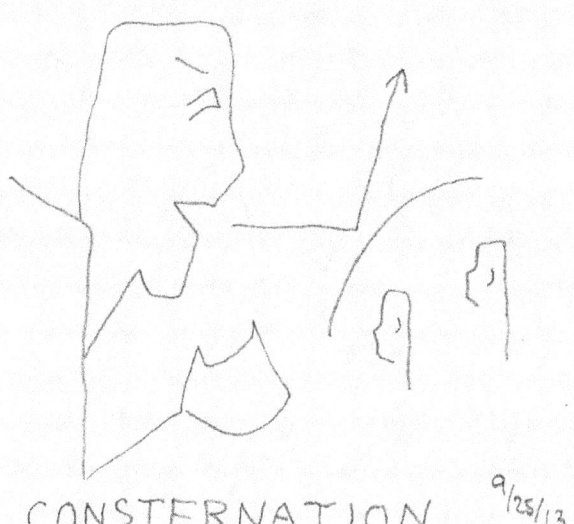
CONSTERNATION 9/25/13

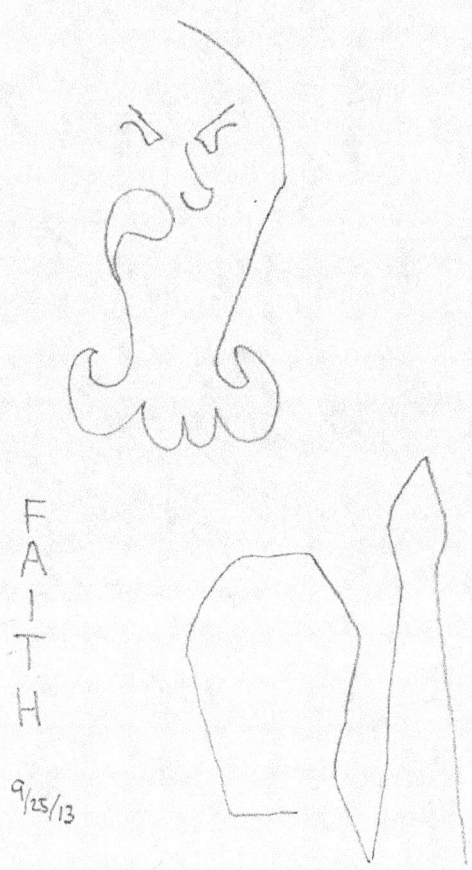

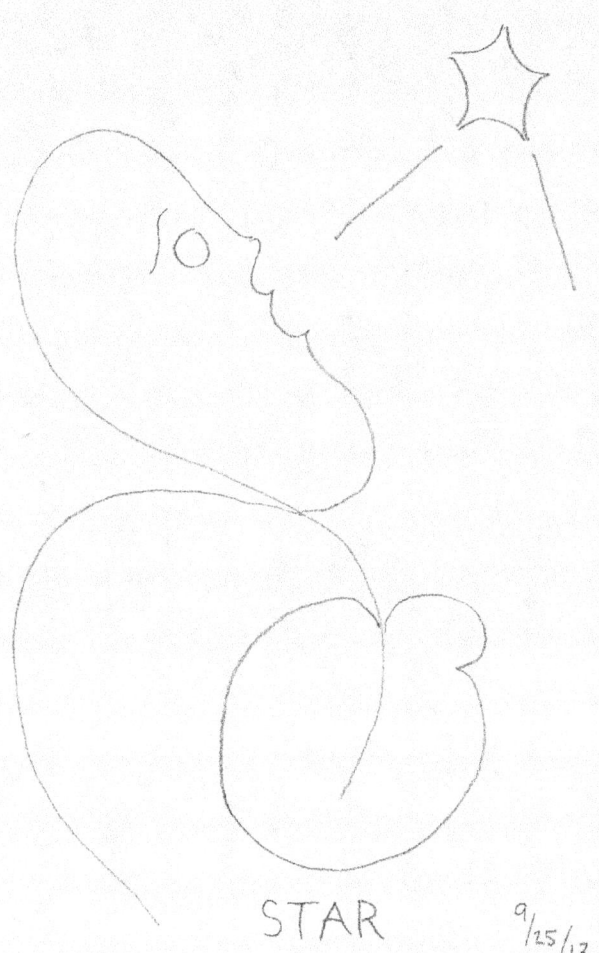

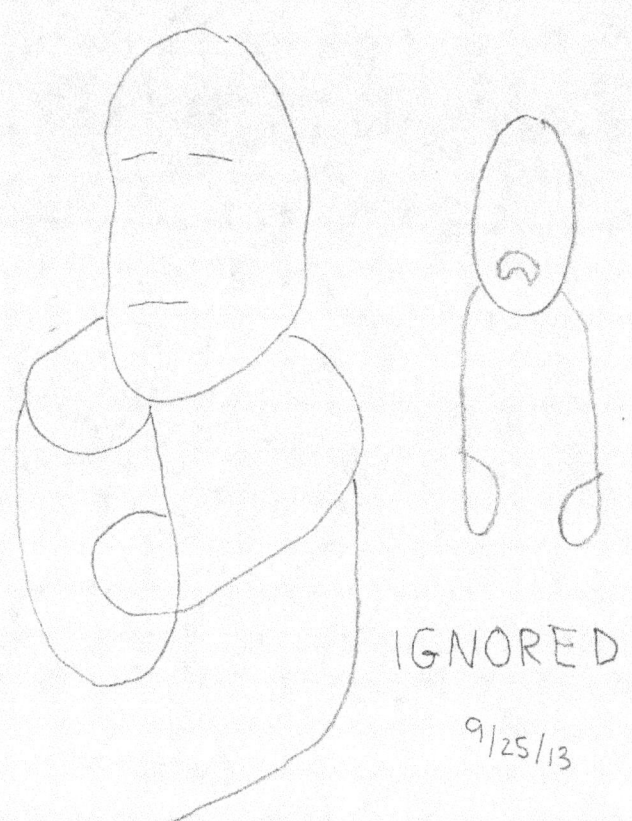

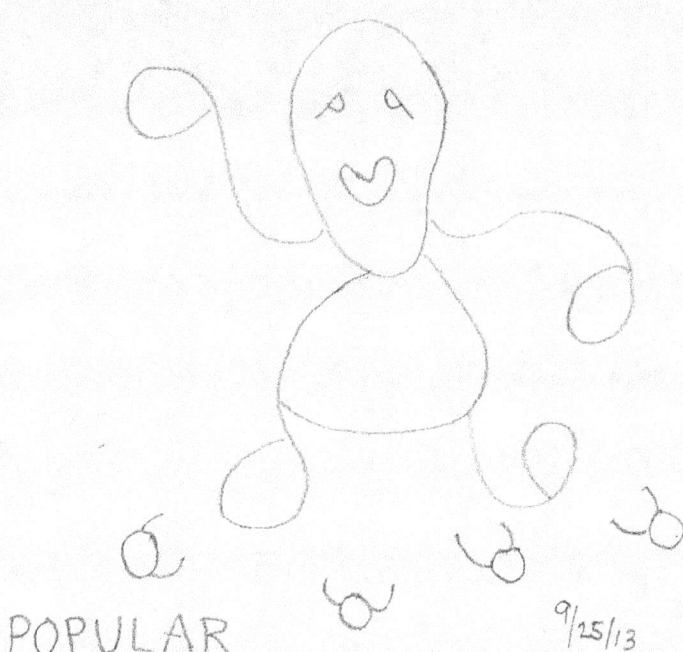

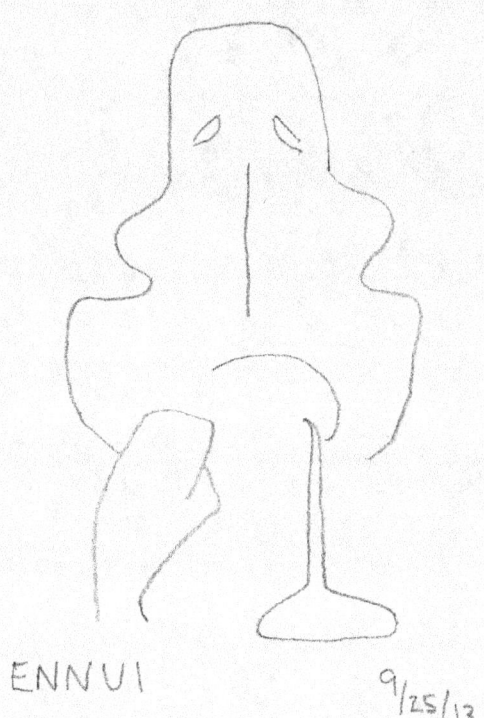

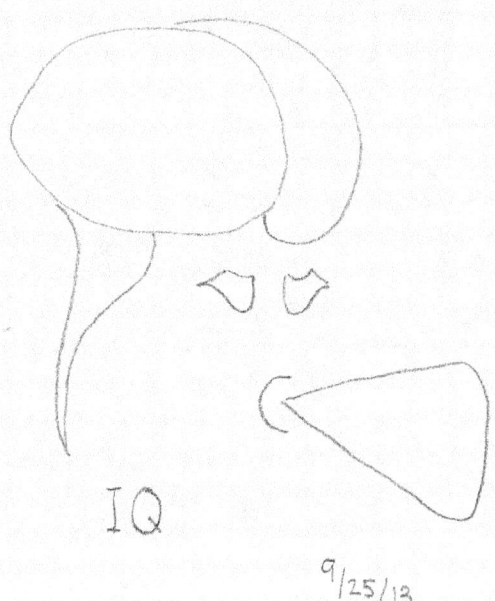

IQ

9/25/13

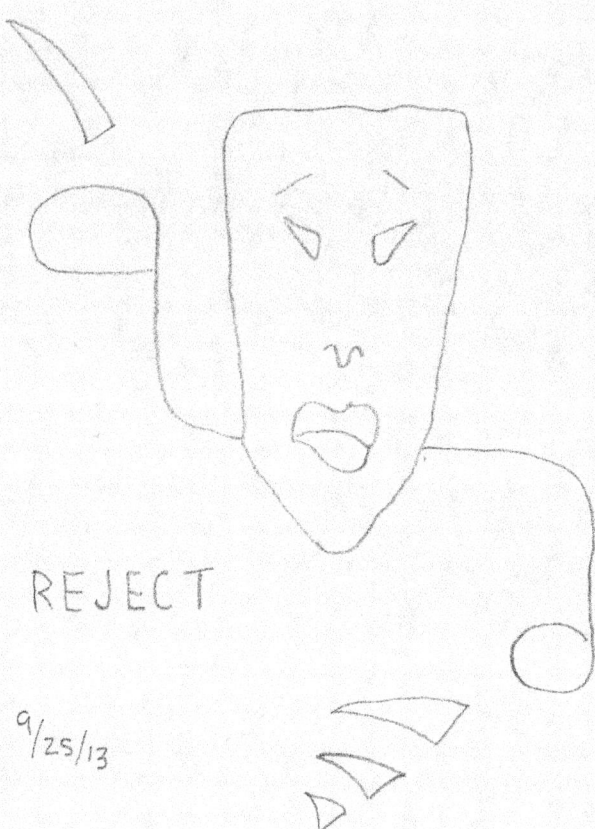

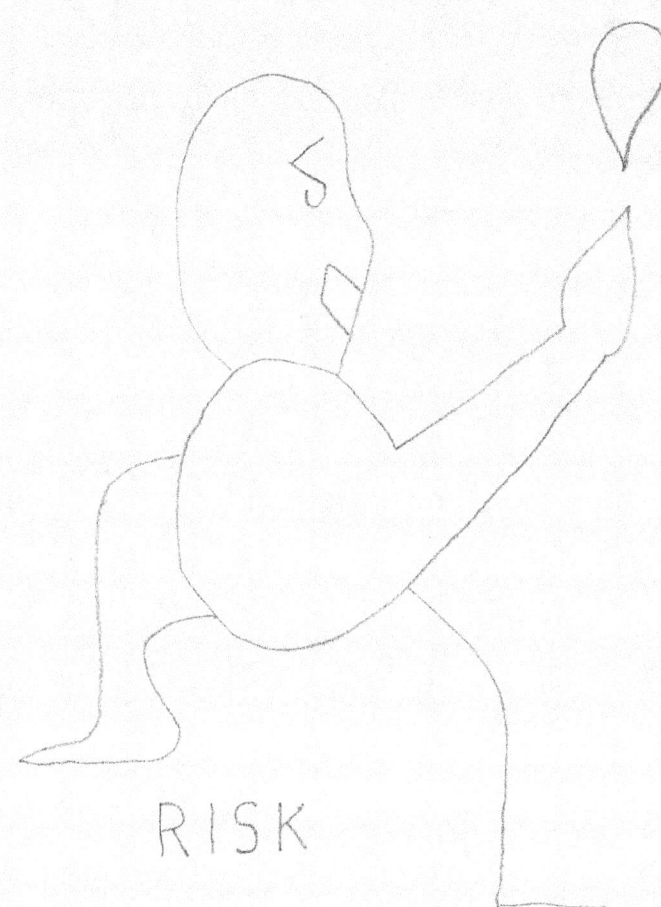

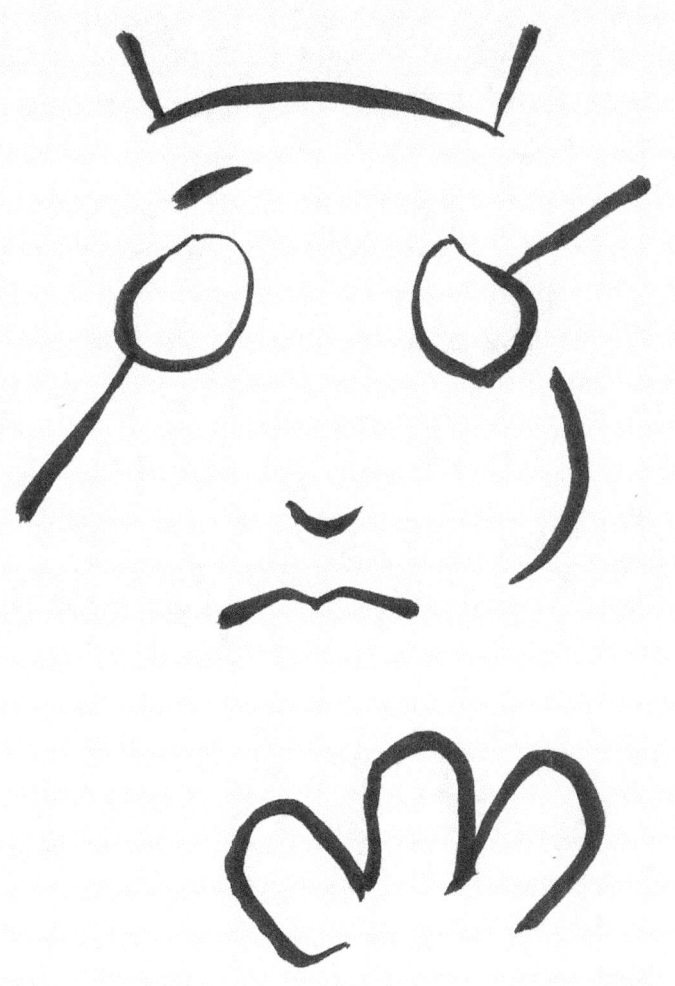

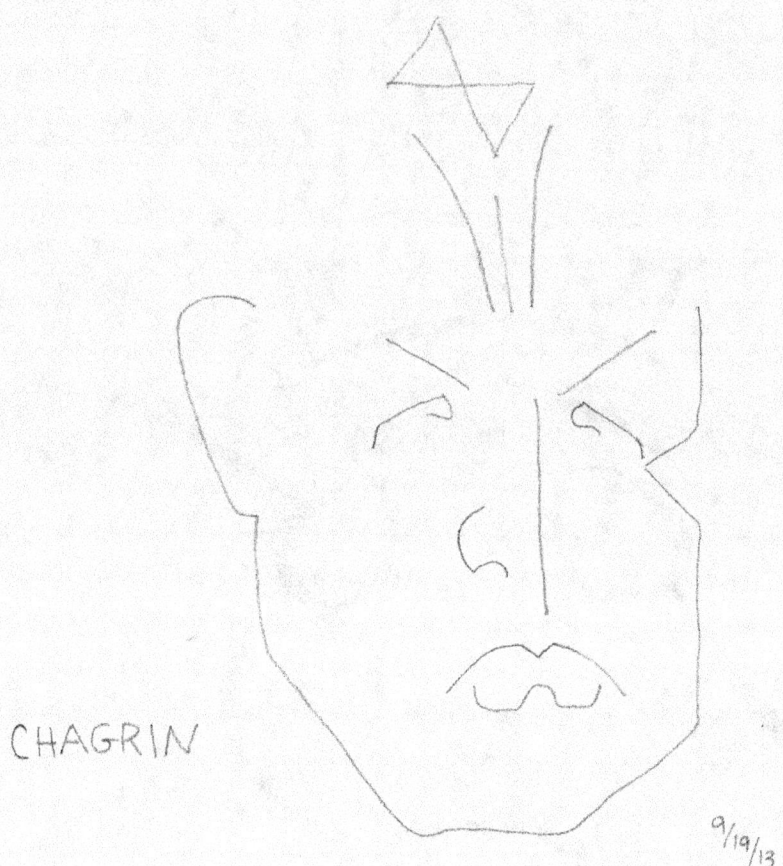

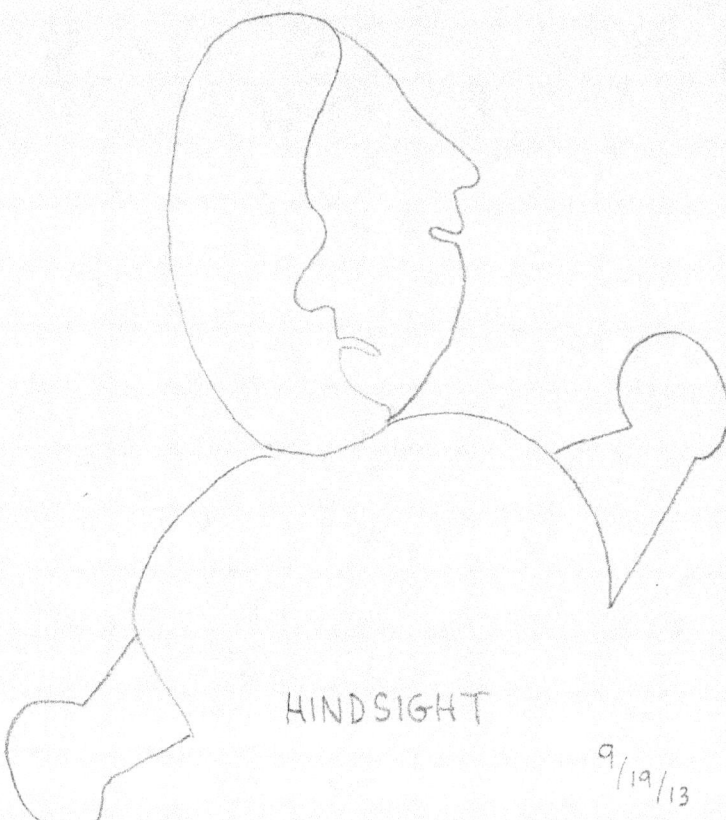

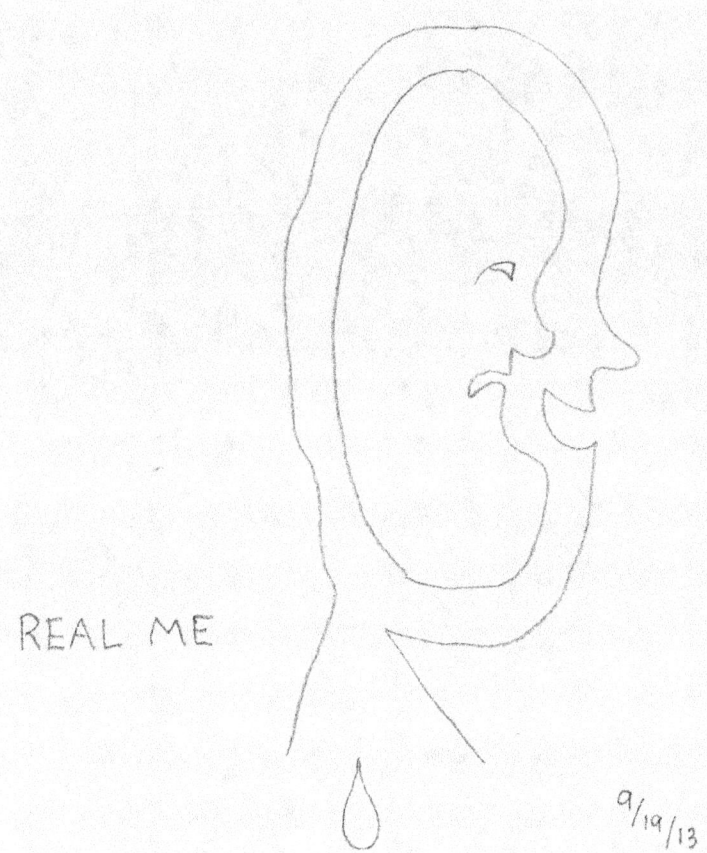

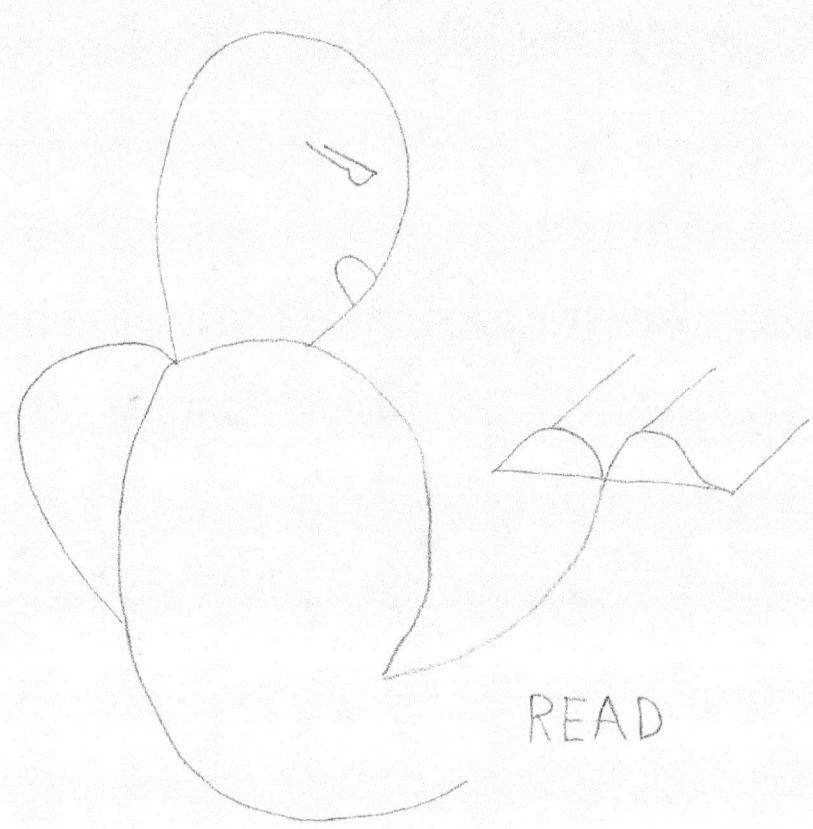

READ

9/19/13

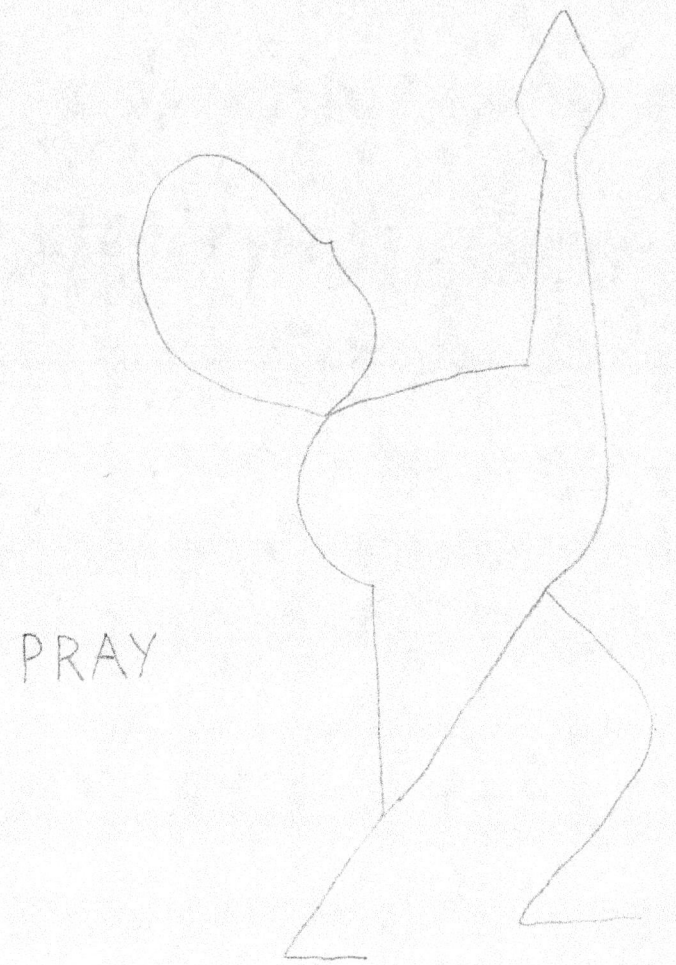

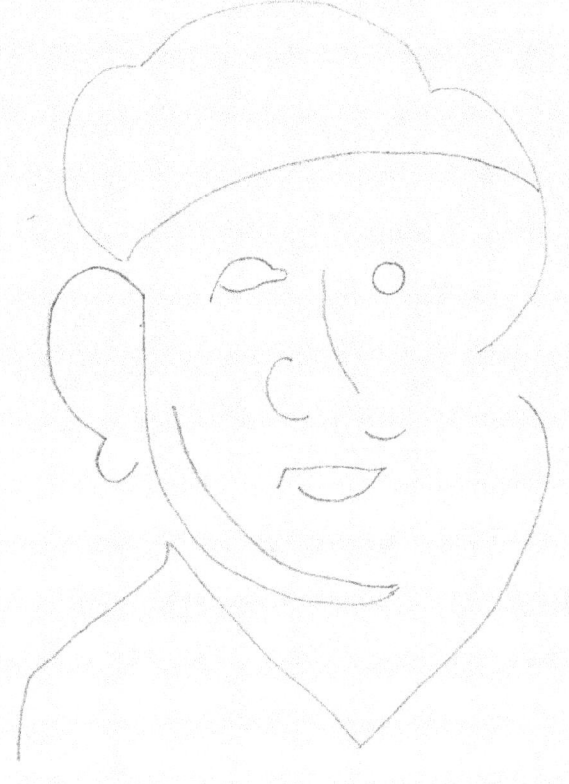

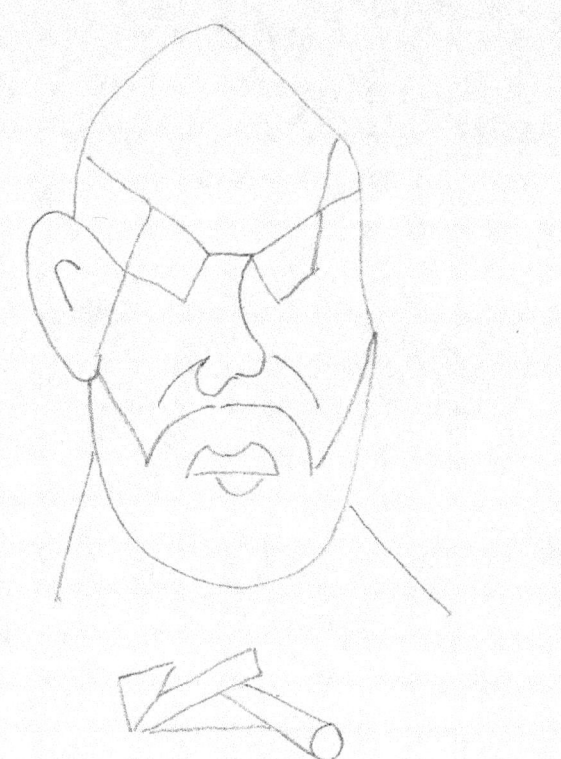

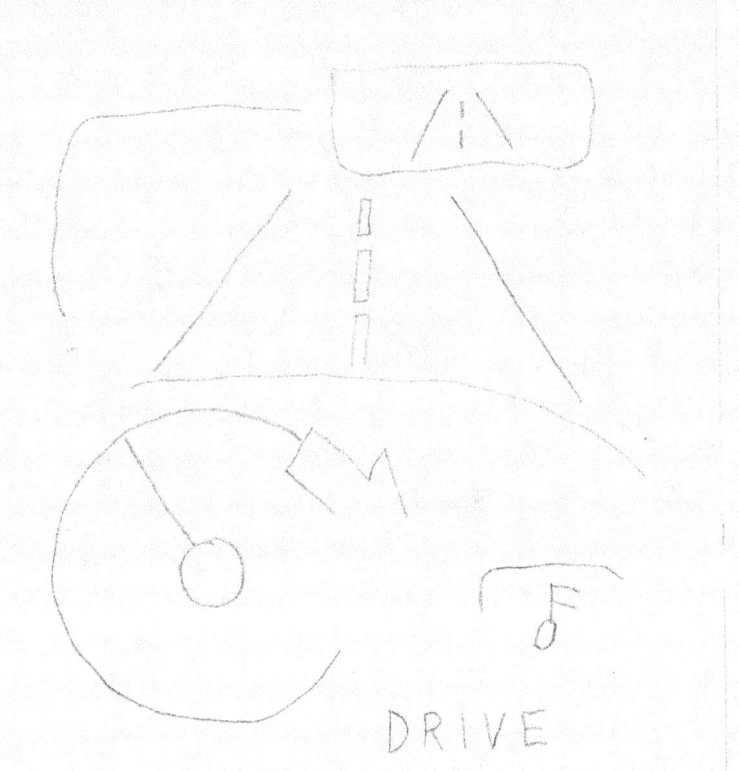

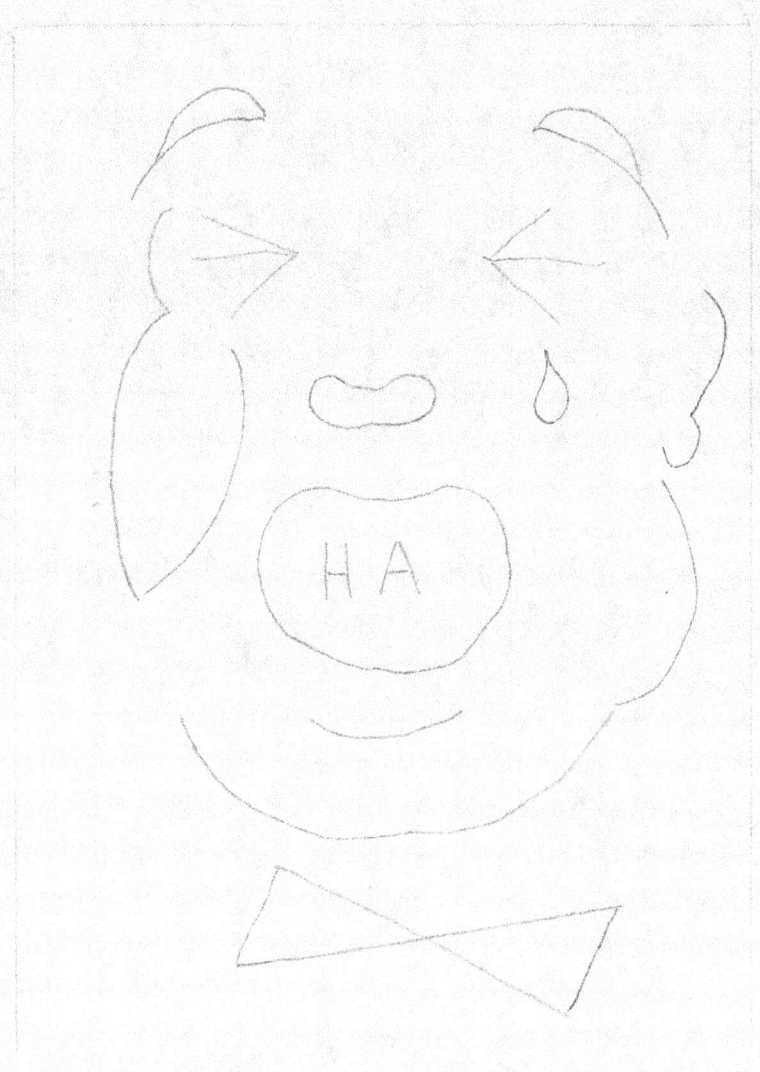

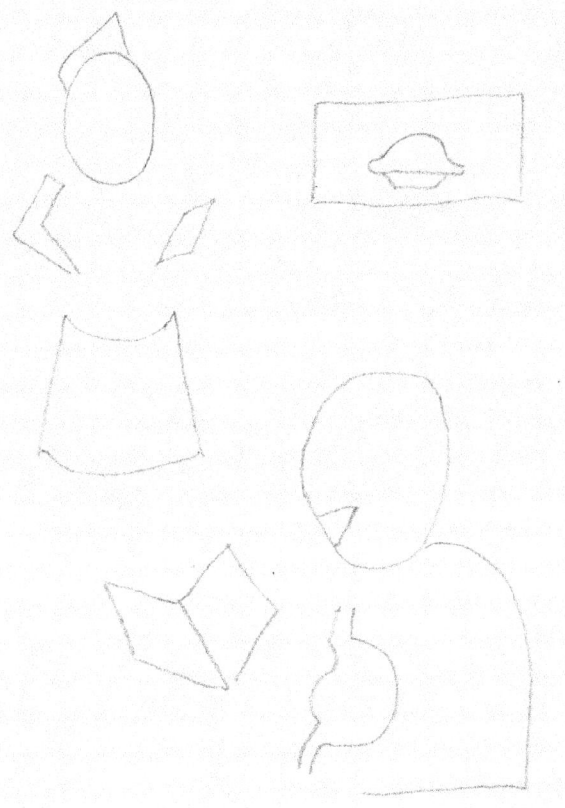

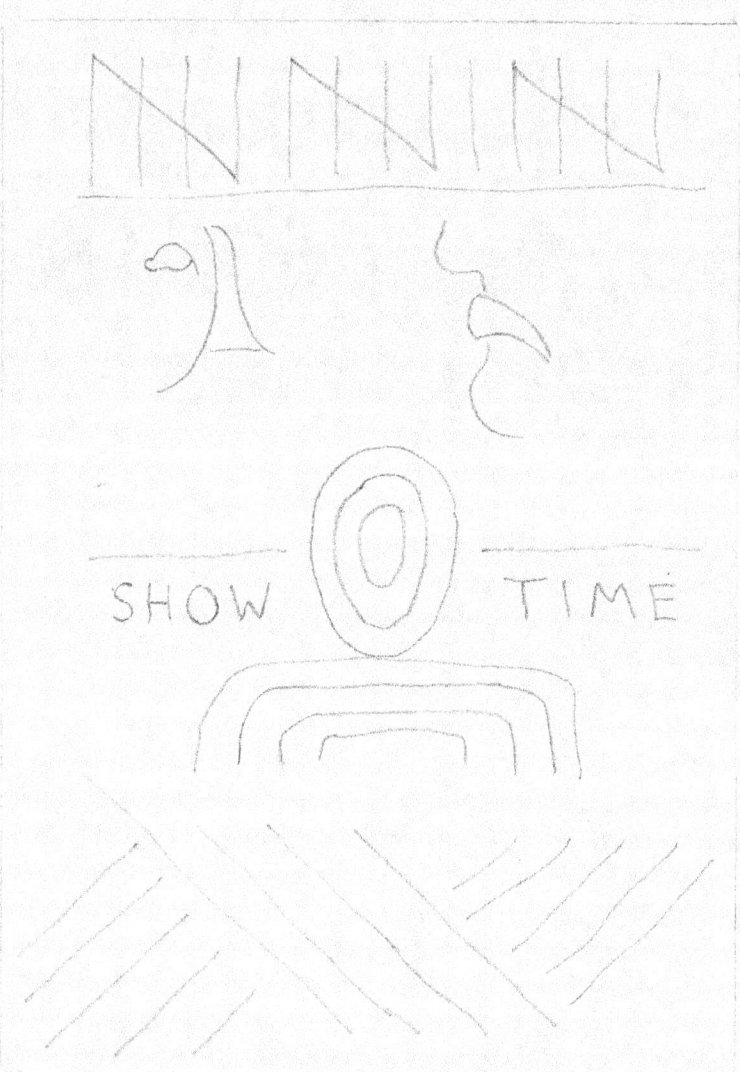

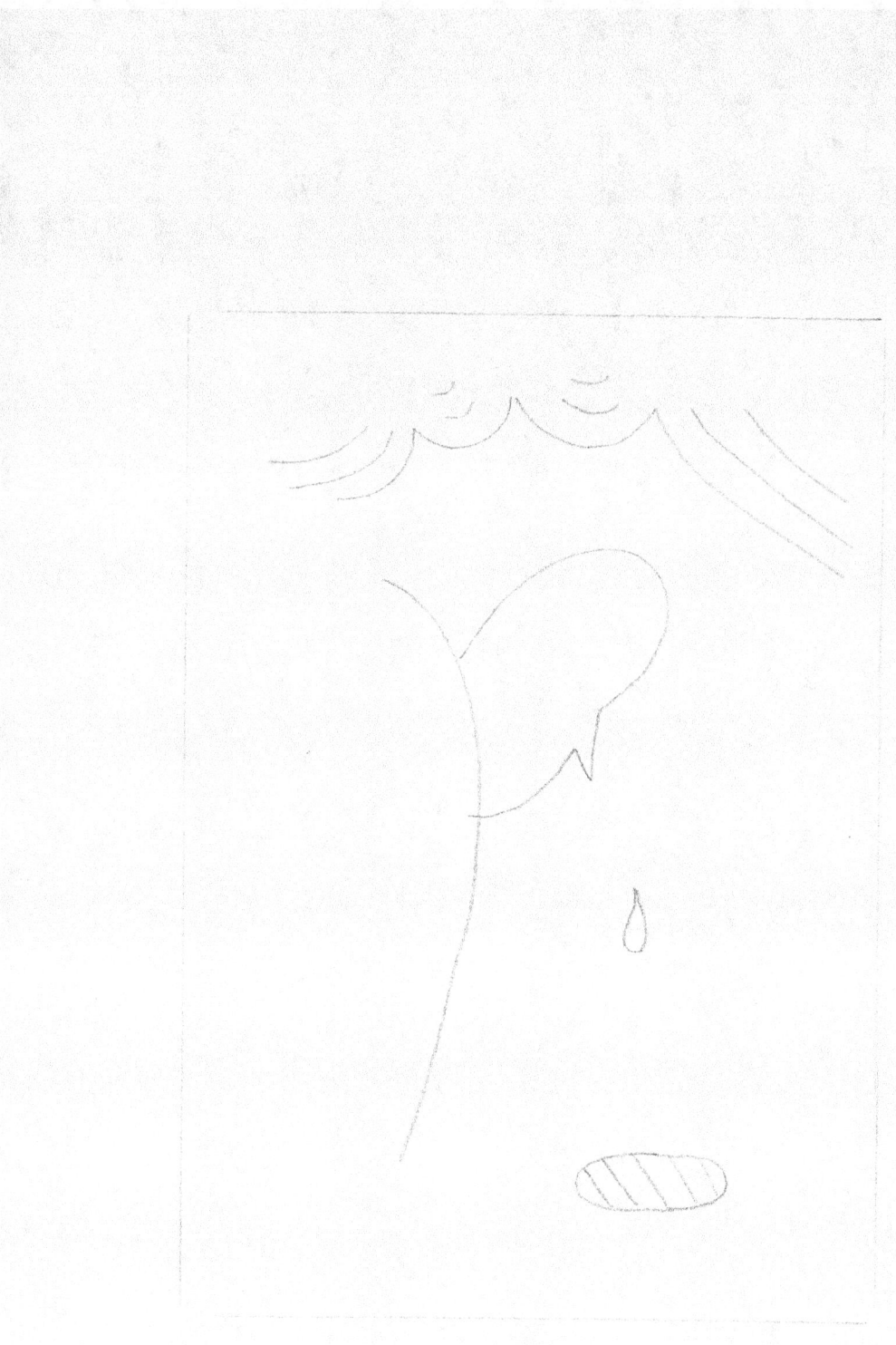

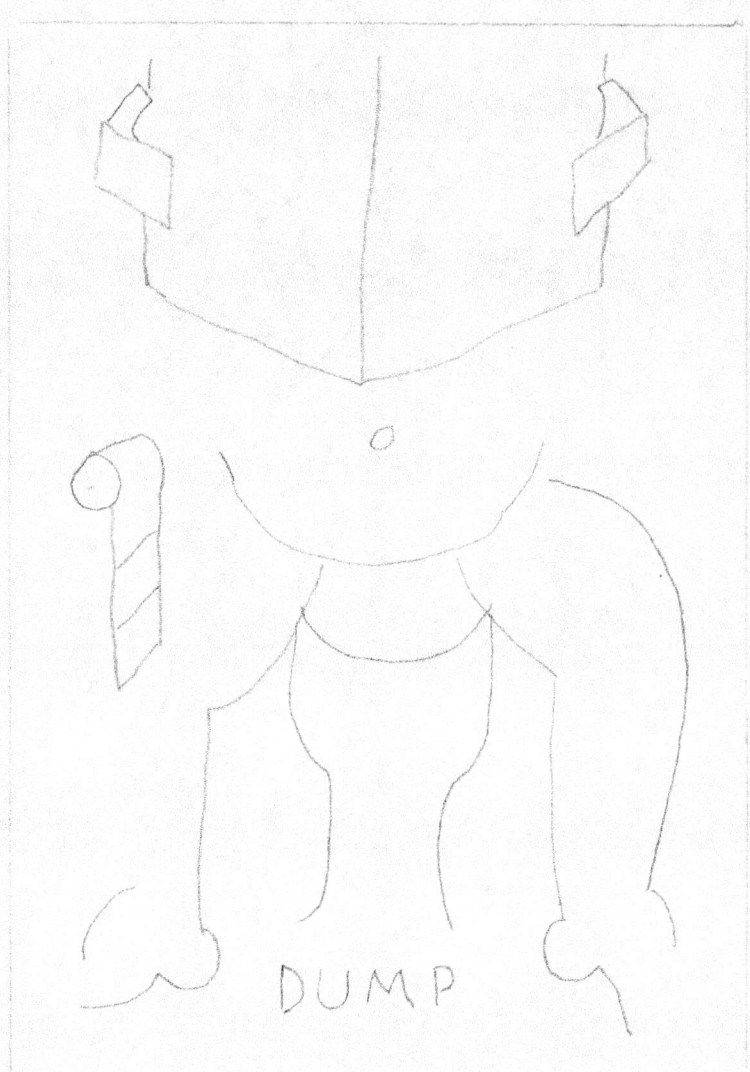

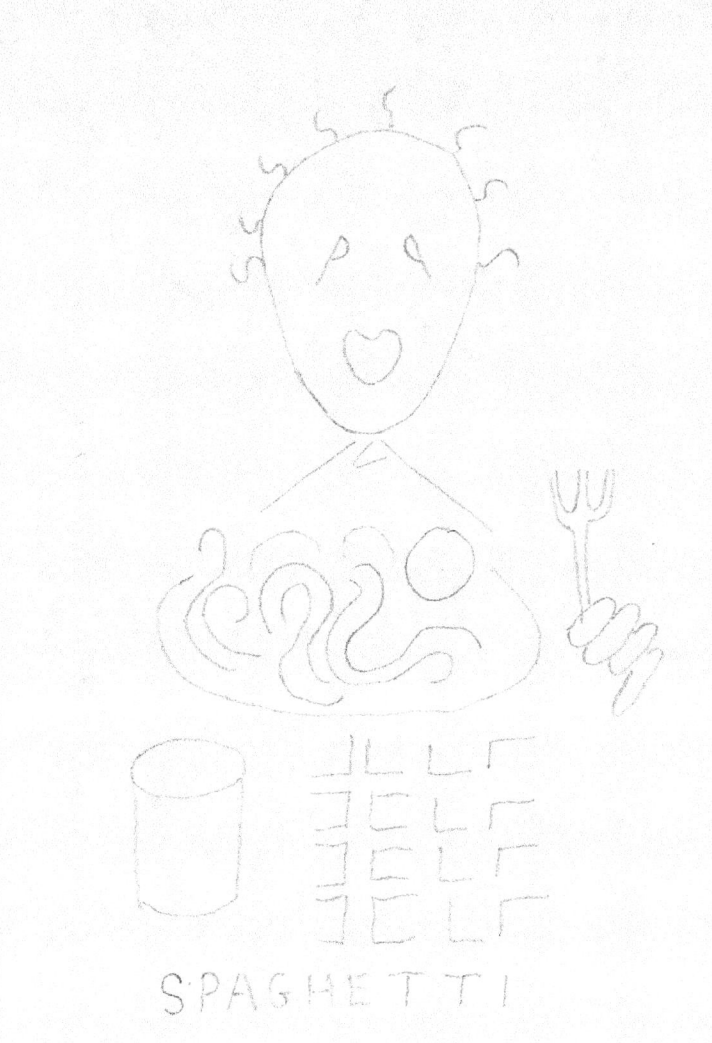

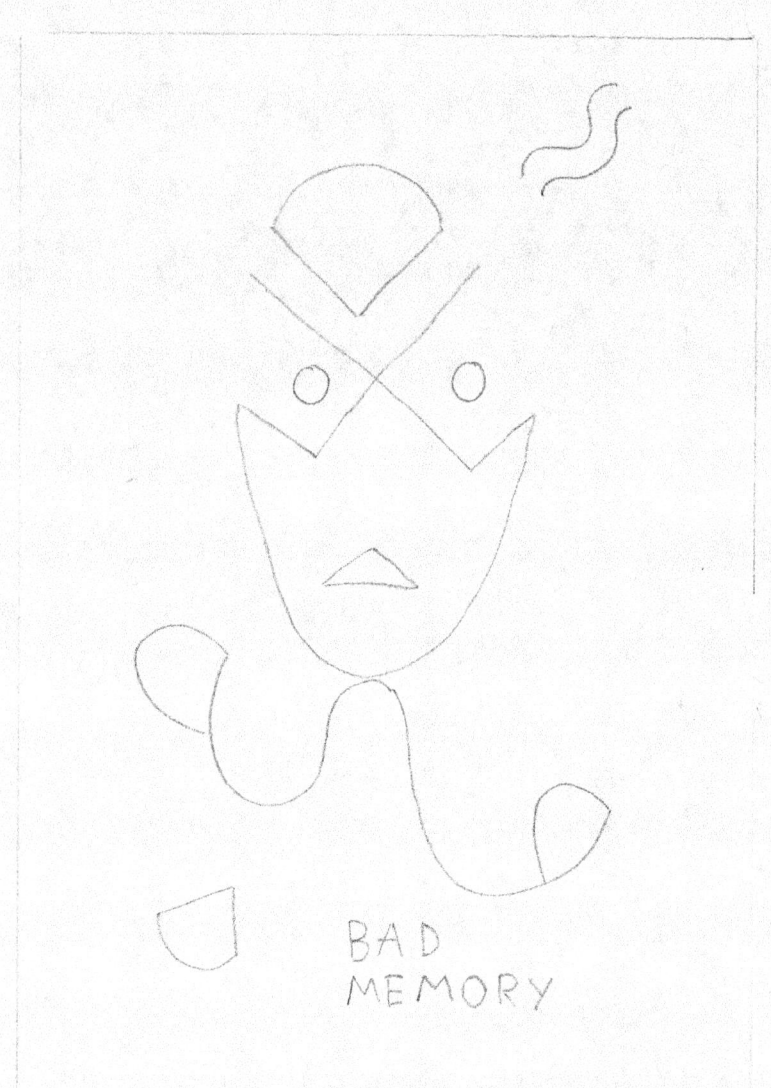

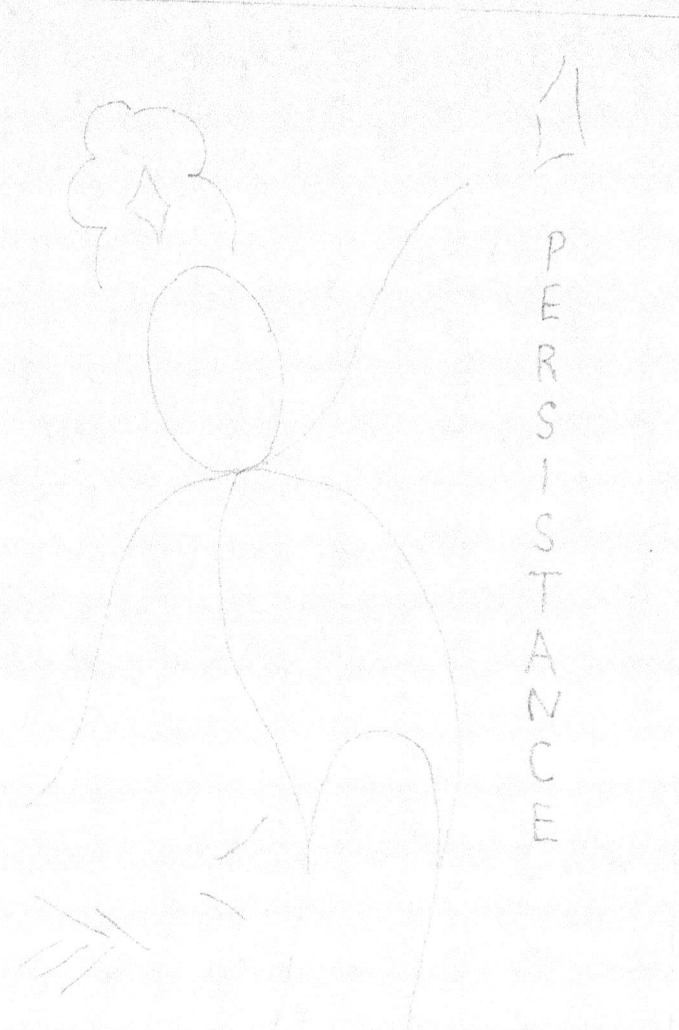

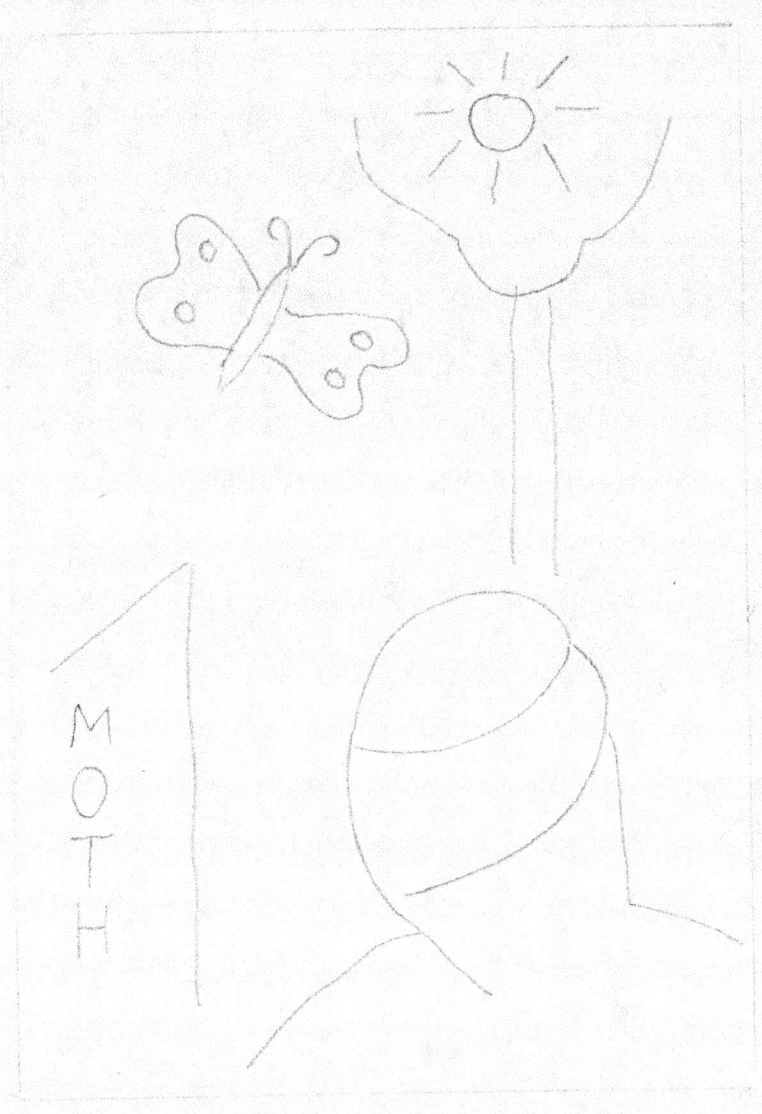

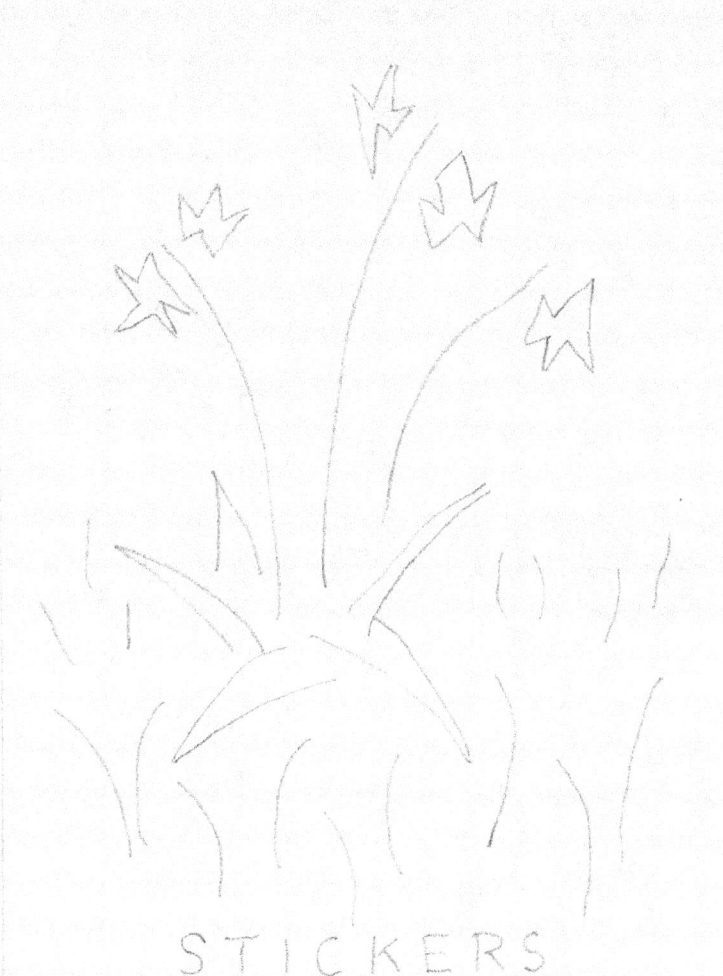

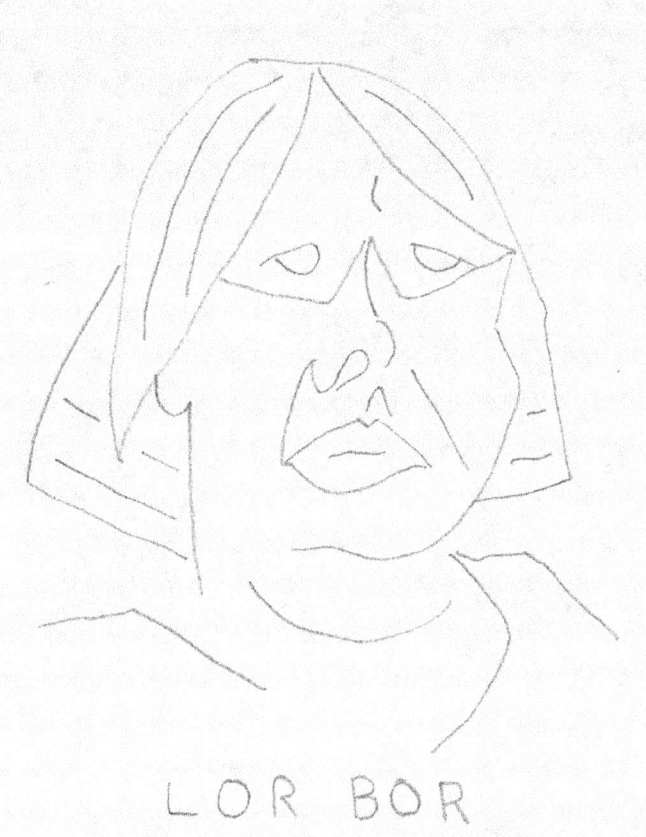

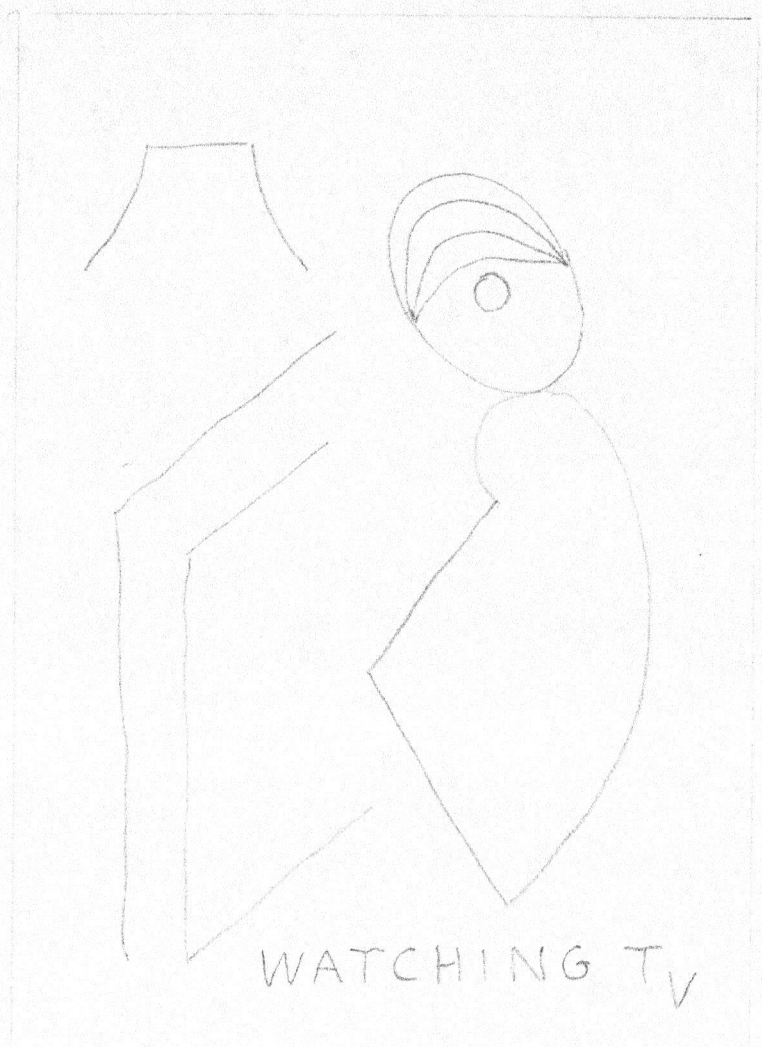

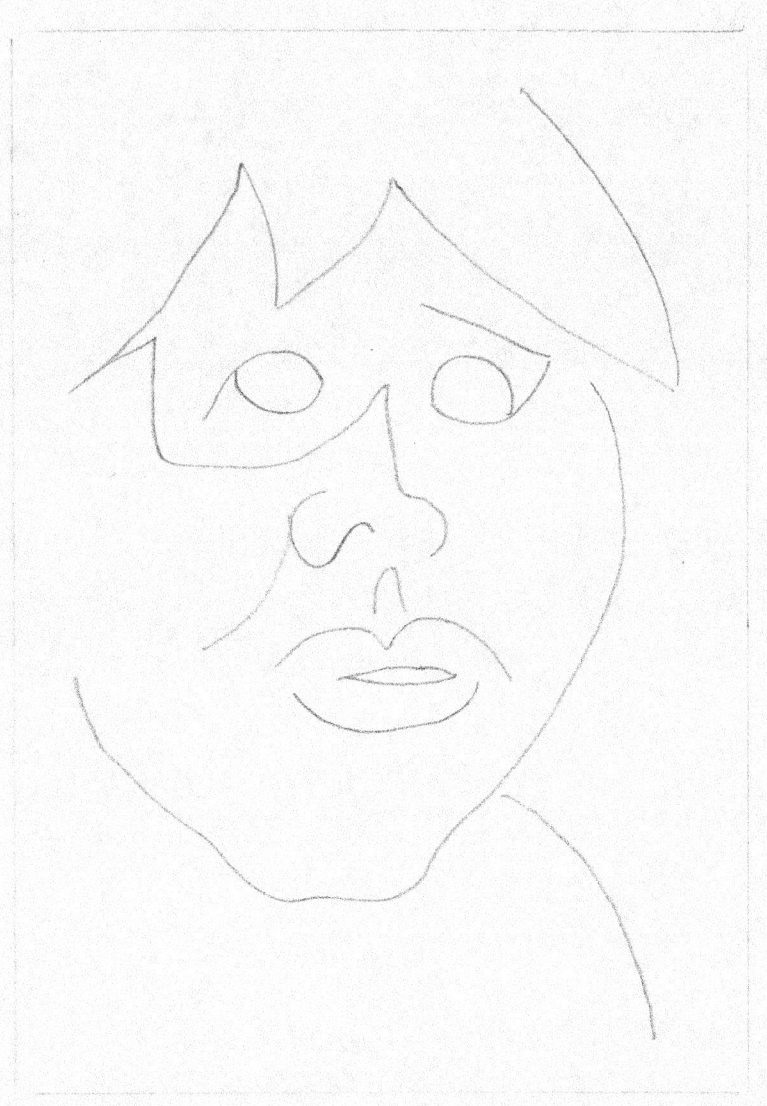

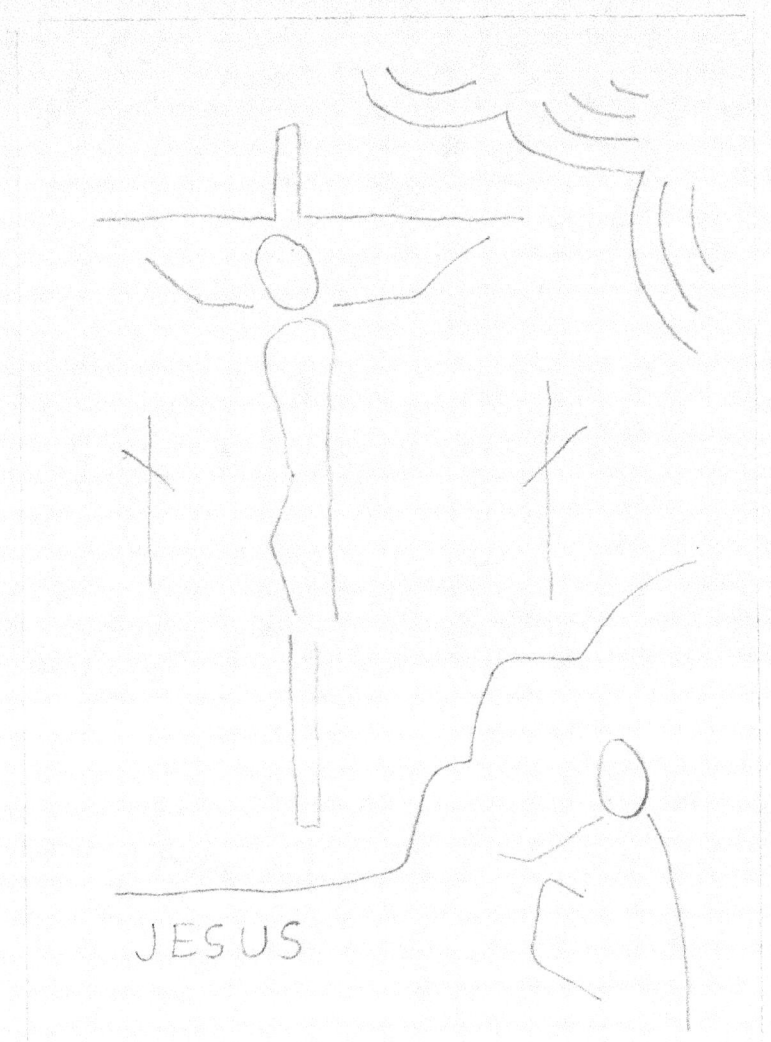

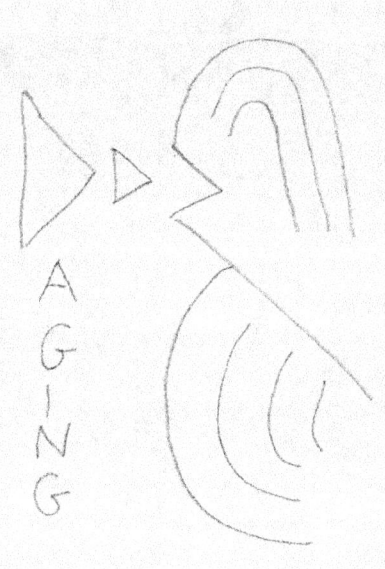

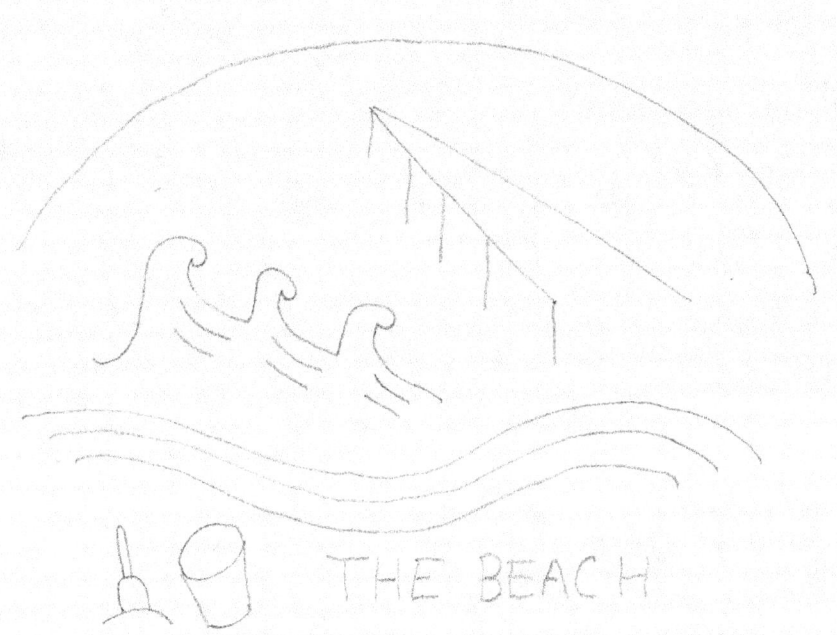

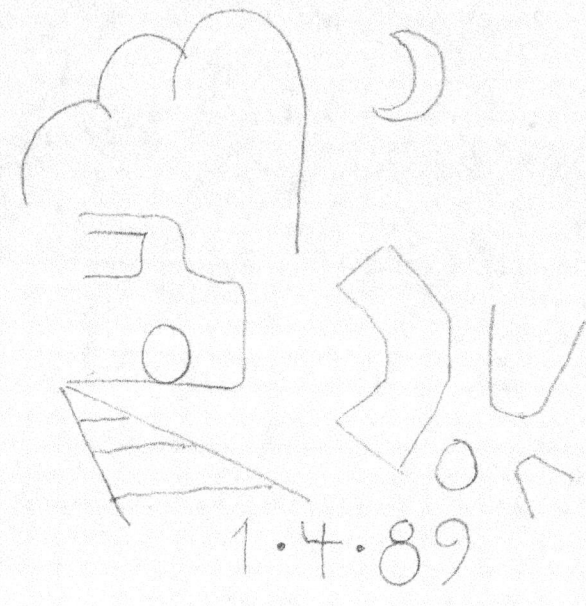

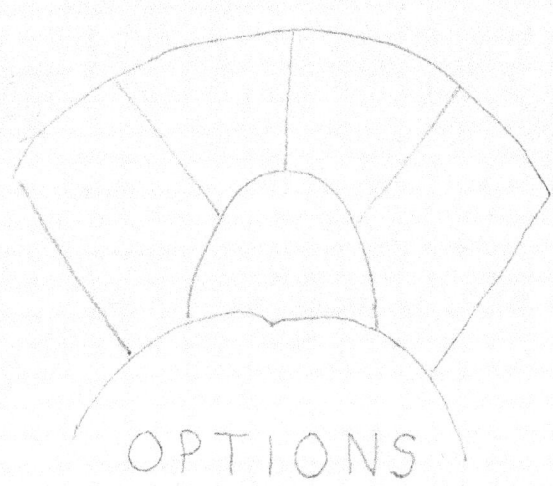

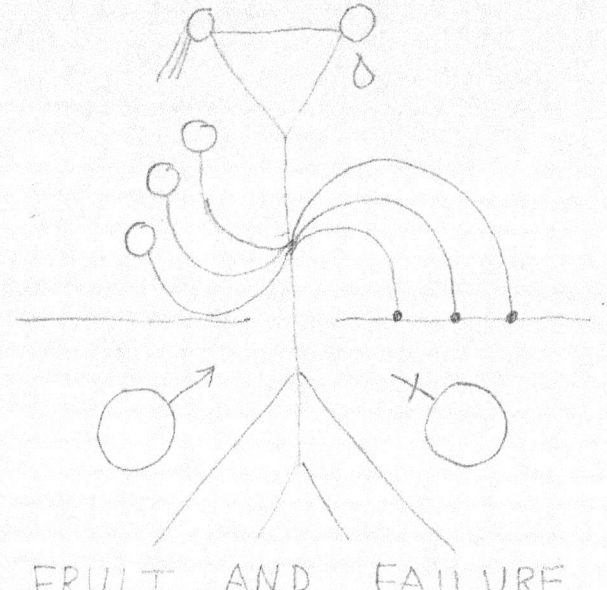

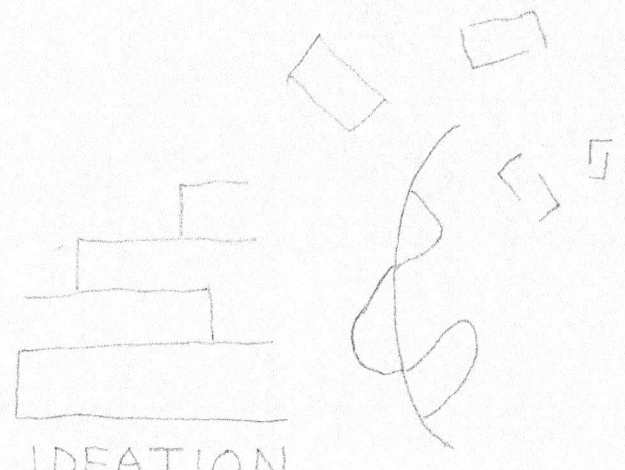
IDEATION

POSSIBILITY

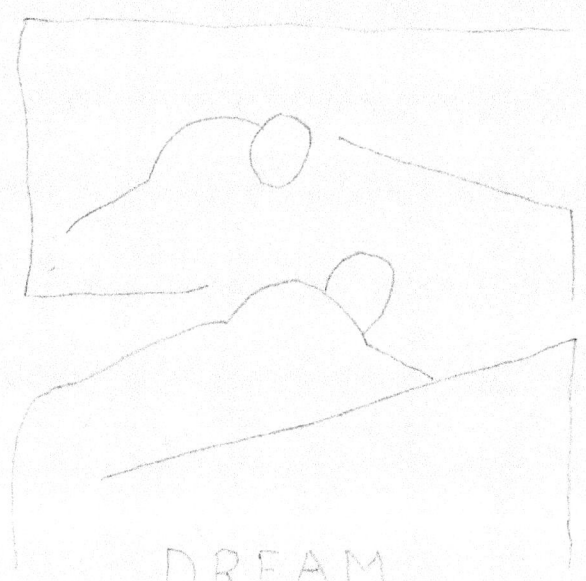

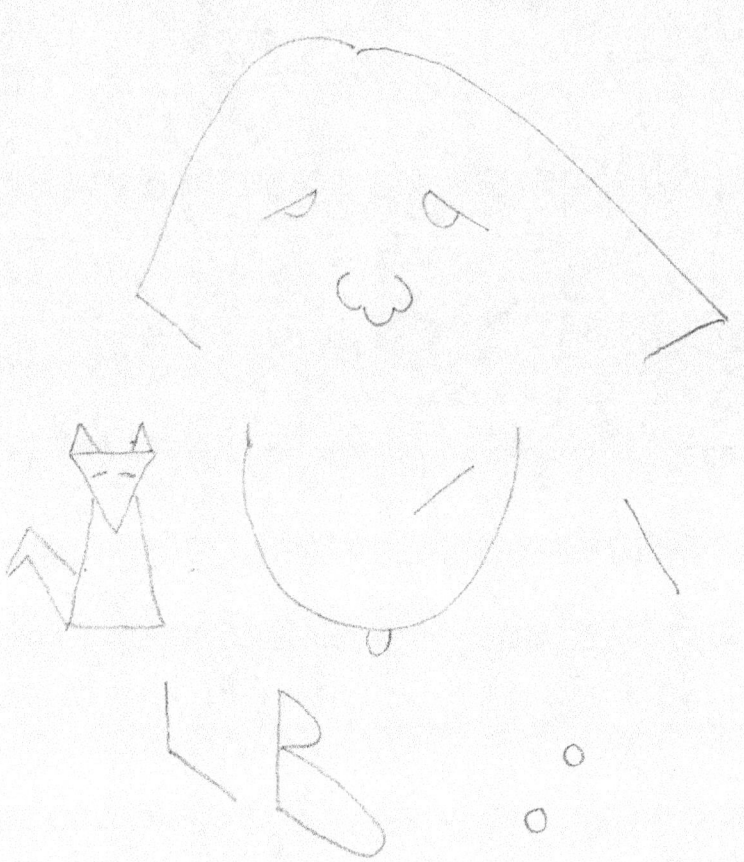

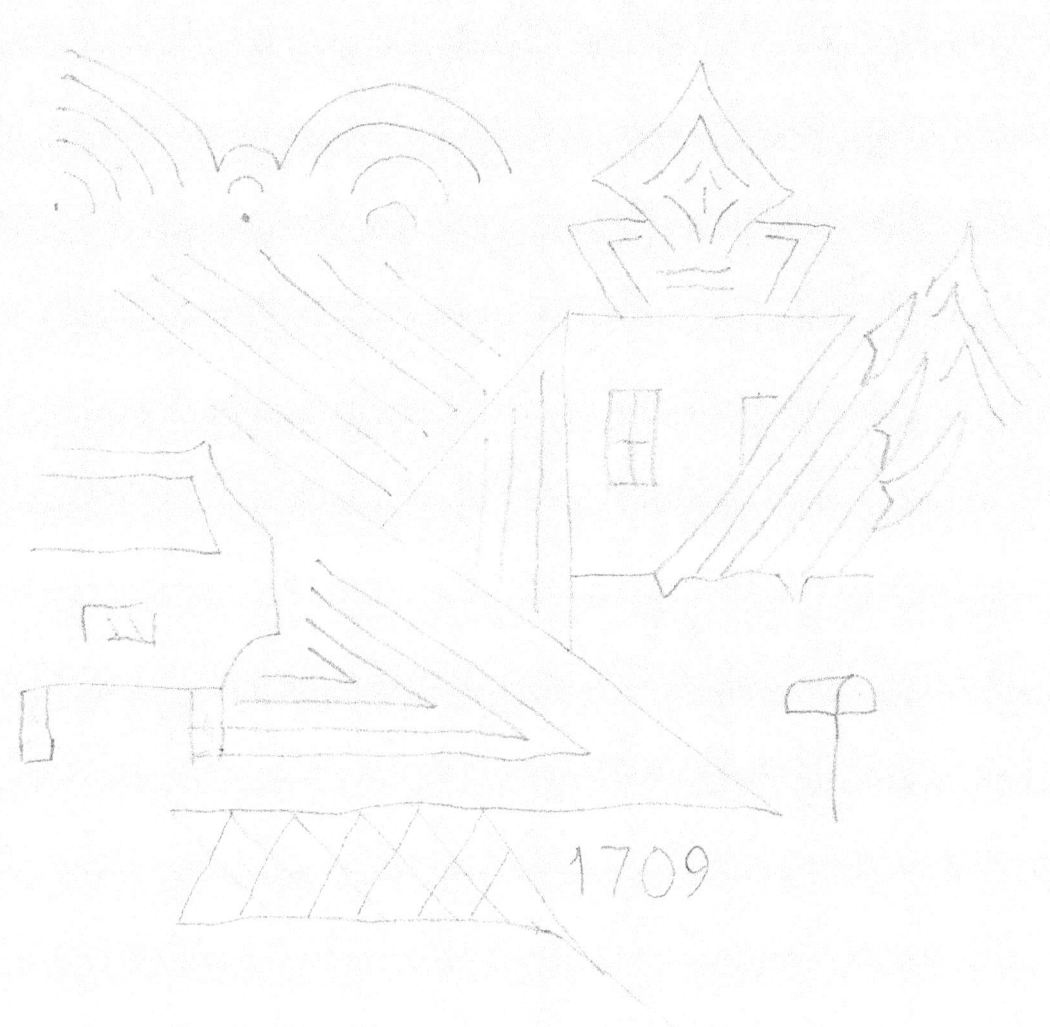

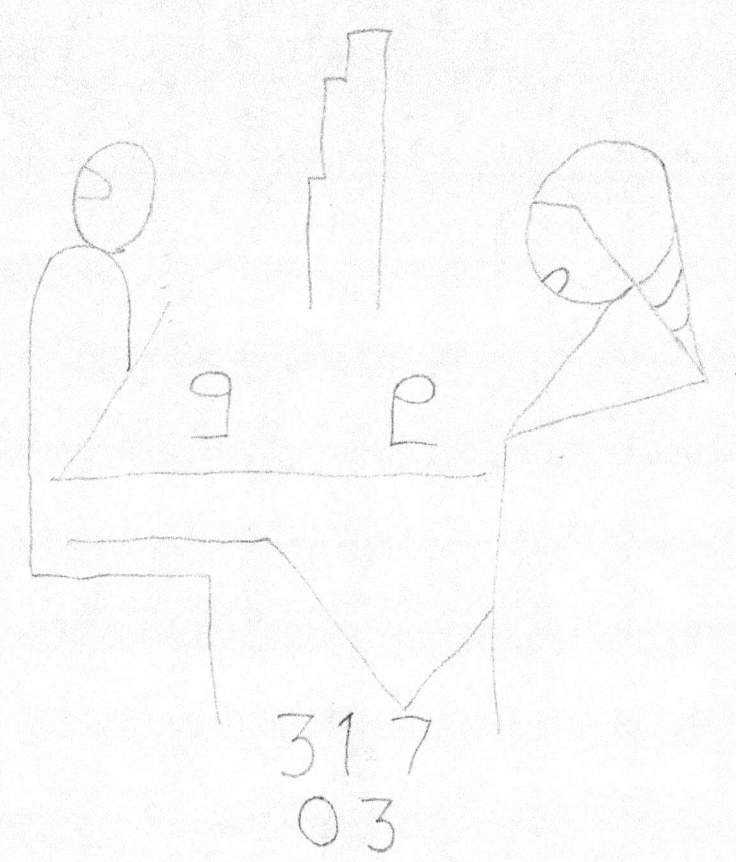

Postscript

KEYES is currently seeking to further develop the original Linoglyphic Art concept which has first concentrated on the singular human experience. Future development of this art form will be subject to the laws of evolution and is therefore dependent upon its fitness for survival in the art world environment. Linoglyphic art has no rare or specialized features, no color, no cultural iconography, or limiting malformation that could hamper its survival. KEYES expects that his linoglyphs will inspire a full range of human emotion and engender broad appeal. Such broad-based appeal should permit linoglyphic art to thrive by reproduction in many different modes.

"I do not know what the next generation of linoglyphs will look like", remarked KEYES after reviewing initial drafts of this book. "I have cast my artist genetic mutation into the art world, and now I must wait for the results. I expect that my genius will imbue this new art form with many opportunities for survival. Of course, it will mutate and perhaps persist for eons, just like… mankind?"

KEYES has retreated into his solitary world of creativity, but has left a small window open to observe the art world. He awaits commentary on this book. The author Bobby Keyes has established a website www.linoglypgh.com where KEYES can read your comments. It is highly likely that KEYES will personally respond occasionally despite his phantom-like privacy. Feel privileged should he respond to your comments!

The author of this book Bobby Keyes, PhD appreciates your purchase of *Linoglyphic Art*. Dr. Keyes is in constant contact with the artist KEYES. Dr. Keyes can also be contacted via www.linoglyph.com.

The End

of the introduction to

Linoglyphic Art...

with more to come!

www.ingramcontent.com/pod-product-compliance
Lightning Source LLC
Chambersburg PA
CBHW080253180526
45167CB00006B/2512